PHOTOGRAPHY HINTS AND TIPS

▲

PHOTOGRAPHY HINTS AND TIPS

BY

GEORGE KNIGHT

FOUNTAIN PRESS LONDON
MORGAN & MORGAN NEW YORK

FOUNTAIN PRESS LTD.,
46-47 CHANCERY LANE, LONDON, WC2A 1JU

First Published 1967
Second Impression 1971

ISBN 0 852 42010 2

Printed by Bournehall Press Ltd., Welwyn Garden City and London

CONTENTS

	Page
INTRODUCTION	8
ABOUT COLOUR FILMS	9
Other factors (10) *Films and subjects* (11) *Colour facts* (10) *Lighting* (14) *Filters for colour photography* (15) *Working methods* (16)	
MORE ABOUT LIGHTING	16
Lighting angle (17)	
HINTS ON EXPOSURE	19
Using a meter (20) *Incident light method* (21)	
HINTS ON COLOUR BALANCE	22
Suggested compensation guide for reciprocity failure (23)	
GENERAL HINTS	25
PHOTOGRAPHING PEOPLE	26
Backgrounds (27)	
'DO'S AND DON'TS' FOR SPRINGTIME PHOTOGRAPHY	28
PICTURES IN SUMMER	31
Subjects in town (31) *In the country* (33) *At the coast* (34) *Difficult subjects* (35)	
TIPS FOR BETTER HOLIDAY PICTURES	36
HINTS ON CLOSE-UPS	43
Parallax correction (44) *Measuring distances* (45) *Exposure factors for lens extensions* (45)	
TIPS ON TAKING FLOWERS	47
Indoors (48)	
PHOTOGRAPHING BY ARTIFICIAL LIGHT	48
Exposure (49) *Lamps-to-subject exposure guide* (50) *Outdoors* (51) *Exposure guide for outdoor night pictures* (52)	
USING FLASH INDOORS	53
Bounce flash (54) *Bare-bulb flash* (55) *Electronic flash* (55) *Guide numbers for blue flashbulbs* (56)	
DAYLIGHT INDOORS	57
Other subjects (58)	
COLOURFUL AUTUMN	59
Sunsets (60)	
FINDING WINTER PICTURES	61
Lighting (62) *Grasp opportunities* (63)	

Page

HINTS ON SLIDE SHOWS 64
Screens (64) *Screen surfaces* (73) *Sizes* (73) *Chart of screen sizes* (74) *Projectors* (74) *Automation* (75) *Noise* (76) *'Popping'* (77) *Projector maintenance* (77) *Successful shows* (78) *How many slides?* (79) *Tips that help* (80)

TIPS FOR CAMERA CARE 80

TAKING BLACK-AND-WHITE PICTURES 85
Viewing filters (85) *Colour filters* (86) *Filters for black-and-white photography* (87)

HINTS ON FOCUSING 88
Zone of sharpness (89) *The right time* (90) *Sense of distance* (91)

TIPS ON COMPOSITION 92

HINTS ON WINNING COMPETITIONS 94
Watch the rules (96) *Print sizes* (97) *Captions* (98) *When to send* (98) *How many prints?* (99) *Specialized competitions* (100) *Subjects* (100) *Guide to subject-popularity in general competitions* (101)

HINTS ON PHOTOGRAPHING ANIMALS 102
Kittens (103) *Setting* (104) *Cats* (104) *Puppies* (113) *Dogs* (113) *Indoor pictures* (114)

TIPS FOR CHRISTMAS PICTURES 114
Christmas trees (114) *Candle-light* (115) *Ghosts* (116) *Parties* (116) *Lamplight* (117) *Christmas windows* (118)

MAKING CHRISTMAS CARDS AND CALENDARS 119
Lettering (119) *Deckle-edge trim* (120) *Calendars* (120) *Attractive combination* (121)

FIFTY DARKROOM TIPS 122

HINTS ON ENLARGING 132
Application (133) *Highlights* (133) *Exposure determination* (134) *Development* (135) *Water-bath development* (135) *Diffusion* (137)

HINTS ON GLAZING 137
Double-weight papers (139) *Metal sheets* (139) *Routine* (139) *Glazing faults* (140)

HINTS ON PRINT FINISHING 141
Knifing (141) *Chemical spotting* (142) *White spots* (142) *Retouching tricks* (143)

	Page
MAKING AN ALBUM	144
The cover (153) *Straightforward arrangement* (154)	
MAKING A 'CONTACT' BOOK	155
Preparing the book (156) *Working routine* (156)	
THE PERFECT BUTT-JOINT	157
FIRST AID FOR LOOSE TRIPODS	158
HANDY 'SPOT' TORCH	159
COPYING ARM FOR AN ENLARGER	161
SIMPLE DISH WARMER	163
DIFFUSERS FOR PHOTOFLOODS	164
CLEANING AID FOR SLIDE GLASSES	166
PICTURE-MASKING AID	167
A NOVEL 'DODGER'	168
IMPROVING PRINT FORCEPS	168
FOR NON-SLIP SHELVES	169
USEFUL PRINT WASHER	169
BROMIDE PRINTS FROM COLOUR TRANSPARENCIES	170
VIEWING DESK FOR TRANSPARENCIES	172
HANDY FLAT SQUEEGEE	173
MAKING A SPOTLIGHT	174
ENLARGING MASK	178
BLACK BORDERS ON PRINTS	179
GUARD FOR FLASH SYNCHRONISATION LEVER	180
SAFETY LOCK FOR FLASH EXTENSIONS	181
AN AUTOMATIC SIPHON	182
IMPROVING A CABLE RELEASE	183
A LOW-LEVEL VIEWFINDER	184
A DARKROOM HOLD-ALL	185
CARD GUIDE FOR BORDERLESS PRINTS	186

INTRODUCTION

PERHAPS ONE OF THE most fascinating things about photography is that it has so many facets. It can be simple and straightforward, or it can be complex and exacting—the choice is yours. The casual snapshotter with his automatic camera can load up with colour film and fire away happily with every confidence; the 'serious' enthusiast can delve deeply into the whys-and-wherefores of photographic techniques dear to his heart. Both can enjoy photography to the full.

It is the aim of this book to offer sound advice and helpful information covering aspects and popular subjects calculated to appeal to beginners and enthusiasts alike. The contents deal with colour and black-and-white photography, the novel and the time-tested; the accent throughout is on the practical, although technicalities are explained wherever necessary. Do-it-yourself devotees should find something to bring added interest to their hobby among the gadgets described, and some may thereby be stimulated to further their own inventiveness.

ABOUT COLOUR FILMS

THANKS TO THE high quality and consistency of today's materials, colour photography is not difficult—a fact which you no doubt have already discovered for yourself—and virtually any beginner can achieve a fair measure of success with his very first film. However, although good results are not hard to come by, it always pays to study the ways and means of taking colour pictures, so that the knowledge gained can be applied to make those good results even better. Anyone who contents himself in merely clicking away in a point-and-push fashion is unlikely ever to advance beyond the snapshot stage, and thereby deprives himself of a great deal of pleasure and satisfaction.

Most people have their 'favourite' film, which they believe gives 'correct' rendering, its colours closely matching those of the original scene; and they have no desire to change it. This is a commendable attitude, in that it allows them to familiarize themselves with that film's characteristics, and to exploit its capabilities to the full, But whichever kind it is, it is wrong to think it is necessarily the 'best'—best that is, for each and every subject and lighting condition. If such a film *did* exist, it would literally drive all others from the market.

Personal preferences naturally have a direct bearing on which make we settle for; some like soft pastel shades, whilst others prefer bright, saturated colours or strong contrasts. There is yet another vexed question: which should it be—reversal colour (for transparencies) or negative film (for colour prints)? Although reversal colour is by far the most popular, negative film has much to offer, and it is perhaps unfair to make comparisons between the two, because by its very nature, the projected picture is bound to have better colour quality and brightness range.

COLOUR FACTS

Reversal colour film is the cheapest form of colour photography.

It is difficult to get duplicate transparencies comparable in quality with the original. So make an extra exposure when more than one copy is likely to be needed.

Colour negative films have greater latitude than the reversal type.

No colour print can have the same quality, range of tones, or luminosity as a transparency.

Perfect colour rendering does not exist, even in the finest transparency.

Colour prints from transparencies cannot reach the standard of prints from colour negatives.

Colour negative film has lower contrast than the average reversal film.

Kodak will make 35 mm. transparencies from Kodacolor negatives (in 24 x 36 mm. and 28 x 40 mm. sizes only).

Out-dated colour films are seldom reliable, either in speed or colour balance.

The 'saturation' of a colour is its depth and purity.

Viewed by daylight, most transparencies appear 'cold' because they are intended for projection lighting.

No colour film 'sees' colours exactly as the human eye does.

The slower colour films are usually reckoned to have a contrast ratio limit of about 32 to 1 for faithful reproduction.

Weather changes greatly influence the colour of lighting.

After an April shower for instance, the sunshine can be startlingly bright and yet 'cold'.

On the other hand, pleasing transparencies can be made from negative film, as well as black-and-white prints, and lighting can be either daylight or artificial because correction is possible at the printing stage. Colour prints made from *transparencies* are usually less satisfactory.

Other factors

Manufacturers are constantly striving to improve their products, and recent years have brought striking advances in both the speed and quality of colour films, to say nothing of subtle changes in their respective colour renderings. The kind of result you get (always assuming that exposure is correct) is dependent upon (1) make of film, (2) its speed, and (3) the kind of light on the subject.

Generally speaking, the faster the film is, the *softer* are its colours, and vice versa. This characteristic varies with different makes of film. In other words, fast films tend to have lower contrast than the slow ones. Some people prefer the type of colour rendering given by the slower, contrasty films because they impart a greater brilliance to colours, making them vivid and saturated; in addition, due to the finer grain, the picture image is sharper.

Slow films are therefore apt to accentuate the prevailing contrast when used to photograph subjects in strong sunshine that gives dark shadows (i.e. subjects with a wide brightness range); for such conditions a faster type of film should be used. If you try to correct matters by deliberately over-exposing in order to lighten those dark shadows, you will simply 'empty' the highlights (sunlit areas) of detail. Conversely, any measure of under-exposure will intensify the blackness of the shadows. This is something which should always be remembered: you cannot 'stretch' the limits of *any* colour film if you want truthful results; though you may, if you are so minded, experiment with it to get out-of-the-ordinary pictures.

Films and subjects

The suitability of a film for a subject does not entirely rest upon its inherent speed, grain or contrast-holding ability—its characteristic *depth* or strength of colour rendering should be

SIX STEPS TO SUCCESS

1. Get to know one make and type of film—what it will do, and what it won't. Reversal film has little latitude, so exposure must be accurate.

2. Avoid the overhead lighting which prevails between 11 a.m. and 3 p.m. in summer, giving short, downward shadows that produce dark eye-sockets in portraits. Hazy sunshine is best for portraits.

3. Subjects in back-lighting can make striking colour slides—especially when photographed from near-viewpoints. Hold your meter close to the shadowed (front) part when taking readings.

4. Colour for colour's sake is not necessarily good picture-making. Shots which have subtle pastel shades usually give more satisfaction.

5. Before you shoot, get into the habit of looking *beyond* the subject—and at the immediate surroundings. Clashing, eye-catching details may thus be avoided.

6. Fill the picture format with your subject—it is not easy to mask transparencies to exclude unwanted matter. Take extra care, therefore, with viewpoints, lighting and taking-angles.

considered too. Some subjects would look obviously wrong in strong colouring, while others would look unnatural in pale colours. This is perhaps the weakness in sticking to one film, or one make; it could well be that you would be more pleased with 'X' film for (say) informal portraits and general shots, but with 'Y' film for scenes that are very colourful in themselves, i.e. flower studies etc.

POINTS TO NOTE

- ★ Don't *guess* exposures for colour; use a guide, or better still, a meter.
- ★ Reversal colour exposures need to be correct within half a stop either way.
- ★ Study the direction of the sunlight, and its intensity.
- ★ Slow film is more contrasty than fast, and cannot cope with a wide lighting range so successfully.
- ★ No exposure meter is infallible without the photographer assessing the circumstances and the subject.

The overall colour bias differs with the make. Agfacolor, Anscochrome and Ektachrome for example, have a slightly 'warmer' tendency than Ferraniacolor, although each has a pleasingly-balanced rendering of pastel shades. There are other variables which can affect the issue: the processing of the film may create differences in colour renderings; there are batch-to-batch variations in the same make and type, and slight colour changes may take place as the film ages.

Much of what has been stated about colour and contrast applies to both reversal films for transparencies, and colour negative for prints. With regard to film speed (at the time of writing) the user of negative stock has only three from which to choose—either those rated at 40 ASA, 32 ASA or 80 ASA. In practice, this still allows a fair amount of subject scope.

Lighting

Having dealt with film speed and make, and the bearing these factors have on colour rendering; we must now consider the effect of lighting. The eye adjusts itself to prevailing light and sees colours *as we know them to be*, even when the actual lighting—colour temperature—may tinge them with blueness (cold winter light and/or deep blue sky influence), or with yellow (evening sunshine) etc. Colour films have no such adaptability. So don't blame your film if you disagree with its colour rendering when you have exposed it in lighting conditions for which it was not balanced!

Daylight colour films are normally balanced for lighting consisting of a combination of direct sunlight, light from the blue sky, plus that reflected from white clouds. The colder, bluer light of dull, sunless days will naturally produce cold, bluish transparencies. Colour temperature filters are available to correct matters: reddish-brown ones giving a positive 'mired shift' (cutting down excess blue content of the light), and blue ones giving a negative mired shift (cutting down excess red and yellow). Useful though these undoubtedly are, it must be remembered that by correcting the colour temperature of the light to suit the film, you may falsify its 'naturalness'.

An evening scene for instance, needs the warmer tinge provided by the late sunshine; removing this warmth may produce subtle unrealism. For the man who wants to enjoy taking colour pictures in the ordinary way, colour temperature filters should not be regarded as a 'must'; indeed, he will probably find that the only filter he need bother with is the ultra-violet (UV) or haze filter. This adds slight warmth to exposures made on dull days, and is essential for pictures in coastal areas and at high altitudes. Many people leave one permanently in place on their lens (for daylight colour exposures), and it involves no alterations in exposure times in the way that most filters do.

One more filter must be mentioned: the neutral density filter. With the faster colour films, considerable stopping-down of the lens and fast shutter speeds become necessary for short exposures in strong lighting. This is not always practicable with cameras having modest shutter speeds; in such cases, a *neutral density* filter will reduce the intensity of the light without affecting the

FILTERS FOR COLOUR PHOTOGRAPHY

Filter	Factor	Use
Haze Colour	x0	To eliminate excess blue tones in distant subjects, and lessen blue cast in shadows.
Neutral Density	x2 x4	For reducing the intensity of light without affecting colour balance.
Conversion A-D (Wratten 85 or R 12)	x2	To allow type 'A' film to be used in daylight.
Conversion D-A (B 12)	x4	To allow type 'D' film to be used in artificial light. Use only when essential—not for general use.
Polarizing filter	x4	Diminishes unwanted reflections; darkens skies without affecting other colours.
Colour temperature correction filters		
Series R (Actina)		(Reddish-brown filters) to reduce effective colour temperature of the light (against blue cast).
Series B (Actina)		(Blue filters) to reduce effective colour temperature of the light (against reddish and yellow cast).

colour balance. An exposure increase is required. It follows that by using a slow type of colour film in strong lighting, neutral density filters are unlikely to be needed; the more contrasty nature of the slower films must be taken into consideration however, in case it does not suit the subject in question. This is something which you must decide for yourself.

Working methods

Turning now to the question of *using* colour film, some interesting facts emerge; did you know, for instance, that your camera lens can directly influence the colour-rendering of *any* make of film you use? Apart from the obvious differences to be expected between say, a coated lens and an uncoated one, certain lenses tend to give a 'colder', bluer image than others—this is irrespective of their performance regarding definition and coverage. Modern lenses are colour-corrected, but slight differences are still detectable.

There can also be variations in their light transmission (amount of light they let through at given apertures or *f*/ stops). So that even if used on the same subject simultaneously, with the same kind of film and shutter/lens settings, two cameras may not give results that are identical in density and colour. But both owners of the cameras would no doubt claim that his was the 'correct' one. All of which goes to show how pointless it is to keep chopping and changing film makes or camera equipment just to try and get results like the other fellow's.

Planned selection—if you are disappointed with your colour pictures—is another matter; and if you haven't yet 'settled' for one particular make, a few simple exposure tests in various lighting conditions with the subject(s) you prefer, should help you to make up your mind.

• • •

MORE ABOUT LIGHTING

OUTDOORS, IT IS USUALLY recognised that the ideal lighting for most general scenes, and for portraits in particular, is *hazy sunshine*—the sun being lightly veiled by thin white cloud. This gives pleasing shadows for modelling without producing harshness and contrasts the colour film cannot cope with. The brilliant bursts of sunshine which often follow a shower can create problems, especially if your subject is in itself contrasty. Yet oddly enough, this lighting condition is the best for recording those distant panoramic views, the air then being cleared of suspended droplets that become haze.

Beware too, of photographing subjects in open shade while this condition prevails, because the light there consists simply of 'sky' light alone, instead of the needed *mixture* of sunshine and sky light. Without an ultra-violet filter (or similar), your pictures will be bluish and cold-looking.

Using the same filter, successful shots can be made on dull days. The lack of cast shadows will not necessarily mean monotony especially if the subject itself has *colour contrasts*. If you choose your locations carefully, the soft light can give subtle help for pictures of people. Fog and mist will provide studies that are attractively 'different', and which will mix well in your slide shows with shots made on sunny days. Rain can be a great picture-maker when there is brightness too; so much depends upon your new ability to 'see' subject possibilities as and when they occur. With colour negative film however, better prints are obtained by exposing in bright sunshine than in dull conditions or in shade.

Lighting angle

The *kinds* of lighting conditions described have an important bearing on the sort of picture you get; the *angle* or direction of the light is no less important. When the sun shines from directly overhead (or nearly so), it casts short downward shadows that do nothing for pictorialism. People photographed in such conditions have heavy shadows in their eye sockets, and under their noses and chins—results that are most unflattering. Top-lighting like this prevails between 11 a.m. and 3 p.m. during the months of June, July and August, and is best avoided.

Sunshine falling directly on to the front of a subject (i.e. frontal lighting, the sun shining from a point immediately behind the camera), casts shadows *behind* that subject, giving a 'flat' effect devoid of depth or modelling. In addition, the photographer's own shadow is likely to appear in the picture. Frontal lighting may be helpful for lessening contrasts—and is sometimes advised when colour prints are needed—but is not considered suitable for pictorialism. Lighting at 45° to the subject is quite effective, and a simple way to check for this in full-face portraits is to position the person so that the shadow from the nose falls slantingly towards one corner of the mouth. This type of lighting is safe for general subjects also.

1. FRONTAL LIGHTING

2. SIDE-LIGHTING AT 45°

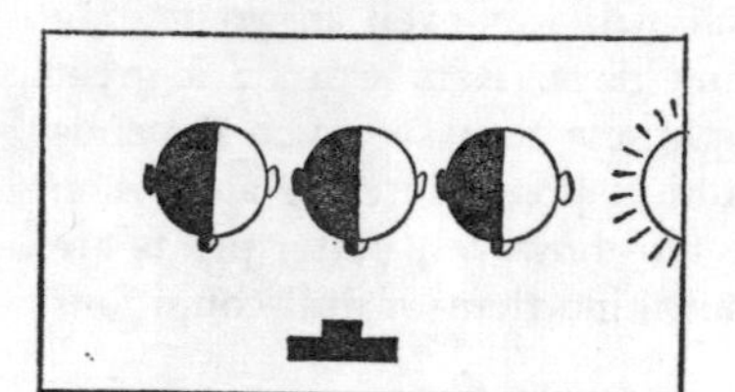

3. LIGHTING DIRECTLY FROM SIDE

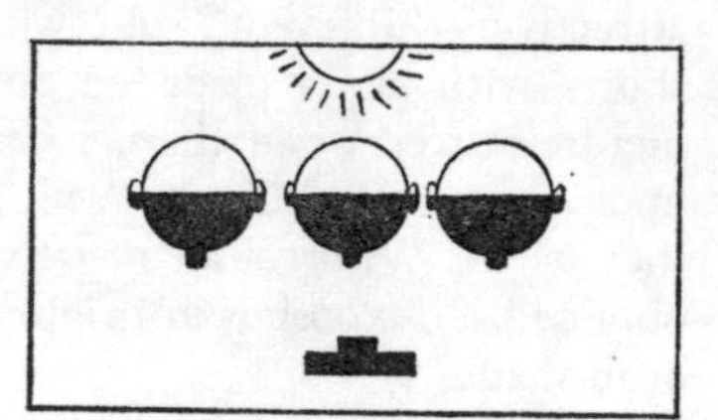

4. BACK-LIGHTING

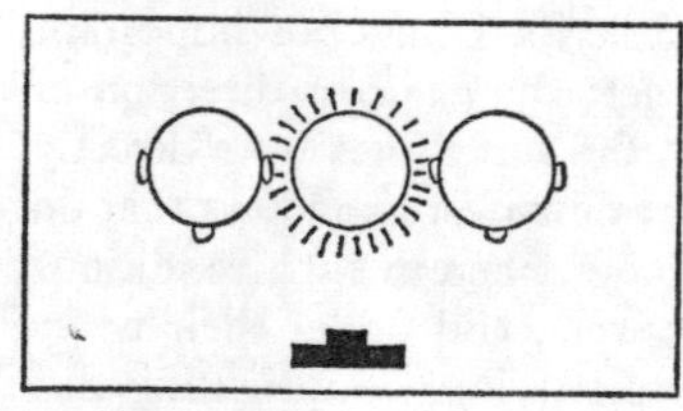

5. OVERHEAD LIGHTING

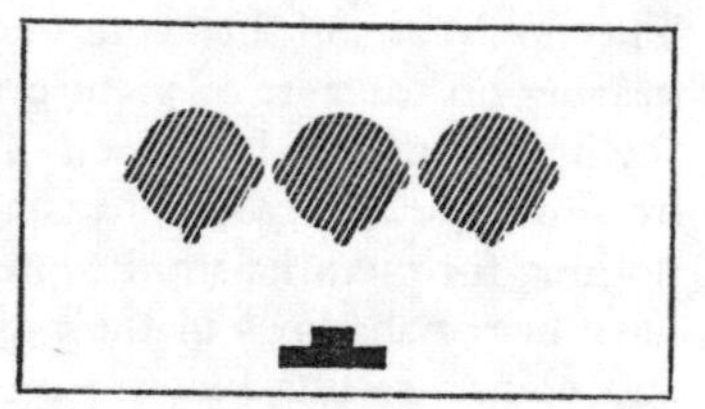

6. DULL DAY (SUNLESS)

Side-lighting (the sun shining from a point at or near the side of the subject), is unbeatable for picking out texture on rough-cast walls, stone, aged wood surfaces and the like, and for producing interesting shadows when falling at low angles. Unfortunately, it will divide faces in two in portraiture, leaving one side brightly lit and the other in deep shadow; so some form of reflector is then needed to lighten the shadowed side—a white sheet, or even a newspaper if it is held close enough, might serve for this. The problem is to keep the reflector out of the picture area. Don't be tempted to use a mirror instead; its strongly directional reflective powers will produce an unnatural effect.

Similarly, side-lighting 'halves' street scenes, giving over-dark areas on one side and probably over-light ones on the other. The contrast range of the film will be strained, and detail may be lacking in parts. Open expanses of landscapes and views from high viewpoints, often benefit by being photographed in side-lighting, especially if there are long shadows cast.

Never miss the chance of photographing a subject in back-lighting (the sun's rays coming from a point somewhere *behind* the subject). For sheer impact and striking results, it is unbeatable. Solid objects have a halo of light thrown round their outlines, making them positively stand out from the background which is usually in deep shadow, while translucent subjects such as leaves, flowers etc. acquire a most attractive luminous quality.

• • •

HINTS ON EXPOSURE

REVERSAL COLOUR FILM has little margin for error in exposure (i.e. it has little latitude). As a rule, exposure must be correct to within one *f*/ stop—an error of half-a-stop either way making no serious difference; remember that over-exposure produces those washed-out effects, while under-exposure gives dense transparencies with heavy, dull colours and loss of shadow detail. In addition, *colour balance* becomes adversely affected.

By comparison, colour negative film has greater latitude, and will provide acceptable results over a range of about two *f*/ stops over-exposure. With this type of film, under-exposure is best avoided, or middle tones and shadow areas will suffer. Slight under-exposure is less noticeable with reversal film.

The printed tables that manufacturers supply with their films can be used with every confidence—provided you are able to classify the prevailing lighting conditions. Straightforward ones such as 'bright sun' and 'hazy sun' present few problems, but 'cloudy bright' to dull conditions are not always easy to recognize with assurance. When this happens (and the subject warrants it), it is advisable to take two shots, varying the exposures to allow for any mis-judgment. Again, the printed figures are often intended for 'average subjects'. For *light* subjects (main areas light in colour) half-a-stop less is needed, while dark subjects require half-a-stop more.

When concentrating on viewpoints and composition, these basic rules on subject tone are apt to get overlooked. An exposure meter, used carefully, pays dividends; used indiscriminately, it has doubtful value. Many of today's cameras embody a built-in exposure meter, either as an independent feature or coupled to the lens aperture ring and/or shutter speed control. Automatic cameras, of course, are completely controlled by the meter, some models allowing manual control in addition.

Most meters are of the selenium cell type (the light reflected from the subject generating a minute electric current to operate a sensitive galvanometer) which can cope adequately with the majority of outdoor subjects. For indoor work, or whenever lighting is dim, the more sensitive CdS type (cadmium cell, which produces no current, but varies its resistance to current supplied by a battery) is better, although a little more expensive.

Using a meter

In straightforward circumstances, merely pointing the meter at a scene and thus measuring the reflected light, will give acceptable results; hence the great success of the automatic cameras that rely on this. However, unless it is tilted slightly downwards or shaded with the hand, direct light from the sky may over-influence the meter. The light reading normally obtained is based on the assumption that the total light reflected from the scene is representative of the mean brightness range of the subject. Obviously this is not always the case.

For example: if the subject is a figure standing against a background of open sea and sky, a reading from the camera viewpoint would probably integrate 80 per cent to 90 per cent of the light tone, and 20 per cent to 10 per cent of the darker—which is our subject-proper. So the meter would indicate too much stopping-down of the lens, and the subject would be under-exposed, although the background would be correctly exposed. The reverse applies if we have a light subject against a dark background. Taking close-up 'local' readings of the subject usually helps considerably, by avoiding background influence.

When using negative films, it is generally best to take meter readings from the *darker* parts of the subject (i.e. 'expose for the shadows', as is accepted practice with black-and-white films); but with colour reversal films it is better to concentrate on the middle tones. This is particularly important with subjects having a wide brightness range: in other words, strong contrasts. It is not always easy to decide upon the 'middle tones' for many subjects—a more accurate method is to take highlight *and* shadow readings then average them.

The slower colour films are reckoned to have a contrast ratio limit of about 32 to 1 for faithful reproduction, and the brightness-range method of exposure determination just described will also reveal whether a subject is too contrasty for the film to deal with. Once you have become familiar with one particular meter and know its performance, consistently satisfying exposures should result; to this end it is worthwhile making practical trials with a film of your choice. Such tests will reveal the true relationship between film speed and *your* equipment, bearing in mind that camera shutters rarely function at the exact speeds marked, and often vary after long use.

Incident light method

Some meters have a diffuser to fit over the meter cell, which is then pointed *towards the source of light* and not at the subject. Measuring the light falling on the subject in this way, instead of that reflected from it, is known as the 'incident light' method. Some experienced workers like to combine the reflected and incident light methods when time and circumstances permit, to arrive at the 'perfect' exposure assessment.

Remember that no meter is infallible without the photographer assessing the circumstances and the subject, and applying its use intelligently, making any exposure adjustments that careful consideration may suggest. For instance; using the incident light method, due allowance should be made for subjects mainly light or dark in colour, otherwise such colours in identical lighting would be allocated the same exposure, when in fact different exposures may really be needed.

When using daylight-type colour film in normal daylight conditions there is no need to be over-anxious about these things. It is easy to become so absorbed by the theoretical aspects of

Incident light measurement

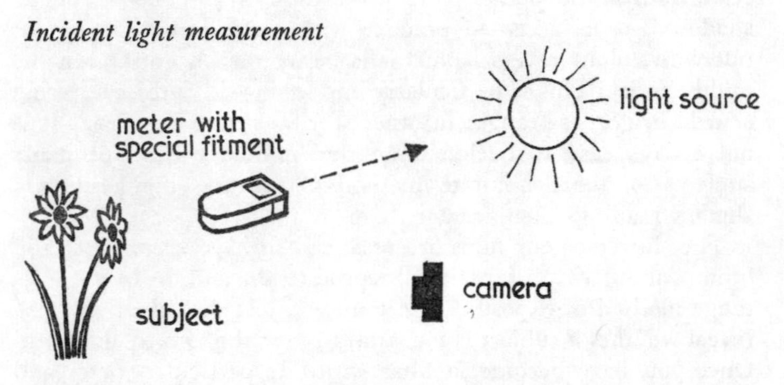

exposure and exposure aids, that actual picture-making lacks spontaneity and freshness. If a subject appeals to you, go ahead and photograph it—don't spend half your time juggling with hair-splitting calculations and measurements! Such delay and indecision may well lose you your subject altogether.

• • •

HINTS ON COLOUR BALANCE

CORRECT COLOUR BALANCE—as well as the density of the actual picture image—can be affected by variations in exposure times. Colour film is intended for exposures of a duration around a fraction of a second; *very short* or *very long* exposures change its response.

This phenomenon, known as *reciprocity failure*, 'builds up' as it were, so that given exposure time increases are not constant in their effect in practice, and some additional increase must be made. By way of explanation: suppose your meter indicated that an exposure time of say, 5 seconds, was needed for photographing an interior; because of reciprocity failure, it sould be safer to increase this figure to 7 or 8 seconds, according to the make and type of film. No accurate guide can be given in this matter, it is usually a case for trial and error, but the following table may be helpful:

SUGGESTED COMPENSATION GUIDE FOR RECIPROCITY FAILURE

(Note: these figures are only approximate, and are intended to serve as a basis for exposure correction. Reciprocity failure effects vary with different film makes).

Given exposure time	Suggested time to minimize reciprocity failure.	
	Reversal film	Negative
1/500 sec.	No change needed	1/300 sec.
1/250 to 1 sec.	No change needed	No change needed
2 secs.	2½ to 3 secs.	2½ to 3 secs.
3 secs.	4 secs.	4½ to 5 secs.
5 secs.	7 to 8 secs.	9 secs.
10 secs.	14 to 17 secs.	15 to 20 secs.
15 secs.	25 to 30 secs.	28 to 34 secs.
20 secs.	40 to 45 secs.	42 to 50 secs.
30 secs.	55 to 65 secs.	65 to 75 secs.
40 secs.	80 to 90 secs.	85 to 110 secs.

Unless circumstances make it absolutely necessary, exposures longer than 100 seconds should be avoided. With interior studies there are times when a 'full daylight' appearance has less appeal and pictorial effect than that produced by a slight measure of under-exposure. Again, if you use electronic flash (particularly units which flash at 1/2,000th. second or faster), you may find that when it constitutes the main or sole light source, the resultant transparencies are denser and less-exposed than expected. This can be due to an over-optimistic guide number claimed by the makers, or by reciprocity failure through the extremely short duration of exposure given—or both. A few test exposures should reveal how much guide-number adjustment is needed.

Colour balance can also change in a film that has been exposed and left too long before being sent away for processing; it is always advisable to have your films processed as soon as possible after use. Other factors which can have an adverse effect are (1) unsuitable storage conditions (hot, humid atmosphere is especially harmful) and (2) the age of the film. Manufacturers print a date on the carton which represents the limit; if kept after this, changes in colour balance and/or film speed may be expected. Sometimes stale film performs much better than it should in theory, but it would be foolish to rely on it or expect first-class results.

Remember too, that although daylight is termed 'white light', at certain times and in certain conditions, its colour balance varies considerably. In early morning, more of the yellow rays are present; towards evening, red predominates slightly. Winter light is more blue than summer, while blue and ultra-violet become very marked at the higher altitudes, e.g., in mountains. Direct sunshine is always warmer in colouring (redder) than the light in shady areas. So if you take a portrait in full sunshine, and then move your model to a shaded spot and take another (measuring exposures carefully in each case), you will find the second portrait to be much bluer and colder in colouring than the first.

Pictures taken at sunset, and landscapes and general scenes taken in late evening, with the sun's rays at a very low angle, can be most attractive; but not portraiture. The mellow, reddish-yellow rays will play havoc with flesh-tones. Your model will reflect those rays, and look an unhealthy yellow in consequence. The trick is to learn to *see* these subtle colour-changes . . . your colour film will.

• • •

GENERAL HINTS

OUT-OF-FOCUS COLOUR, if at all bright, can be most irritating when projected onto a screen. When it occurs in the foreground of a picture it can be intolerable. While all-over sharpness is not always essential or even desirable, extra care is necessary to ensure that off-sharp areas have subdued, soft colouring whenever possible. Fuzzy backgrounds with strongly-coloured elements will force attention to those parts, to the detriment of the actual subject, no matter how attractive this may be in itself.

Avoid having large areas of strong, contrasting colours in one picture; some of the most successful results have been achieved by photographing scenes seemingly lacking in colour, their subtle pastel shades creating a more satisfying appeal than sheer blatant colour. Generally speaking, it is best to keep bright colours away from the edges of a picture, as they tend to draw the eye out of the 'frame'.

As objects recede into the distance, their colours get cooler and bluer. From this, it follows that cold colours—such as blues and greens—recede, and warm ones (such as red, orange, yellow and brown) advance. Therefore by keeping the warm colours in the foreground of any composition, and the cold tones in the background, the greater will be the illusion of depth; reverse this order, and a definite feeling of unnaturalness will be introduced.

By including a person dressed in warm colours near a main point of interest in the foreground, the effect of distance is enhanced. The *stronger* (more saturated) colours are in hue, the more they appear to advance or recede as the case may be.

A compositional arrangement which 'reads' from left to right is usually more satisfying and acceptable than one in which the

eye is drawn in the reverse direction. This is probably because unconsciously we view our pictures in the same direction as we read print.

Beware of colours which clash when near each other, especially if they are at all brilliant. Bright red and green side by side can easily become too assertive, as can yellow and blue, while vivid red next to vivid blue can be positively glaring. Even worse effects are produced when blue-green is close to blue, or vermilion near to magenta. It is a question of some colours 'going' with others, and vice versa. Some people have a flair for colour, and can sense subtle blendings, contrasts and clashes, more readily than others.

If you are working with two cameras, one loaded with colour, and the other with black-and-white film, you may well find that the technique for the one is apt to become fused into that for the other, with unfortunate results for both. This is because a good subject for colour is not always a good one for black-and-white; it is in fact more difficult to recognise likely pictorial material for monochrome film.

Rule-of-thumb methods for compositional arrangement can do much to set you on the right road until you are able to instinctively select pleasing viewpoints etc.; until you reach this stage, it is better not to ignore the basic 'rules'—it might prove expensive in terms of wasted colour film! There are no short cuts to success, but whatever your subject, you will generally find that it pays to stick to the old adage: *keep it simple.*

• • •

PHOTOGRAPHING PEOPLE

THERE IS ALWAYS A strong temptation to get too close with the camera when photographing people; head-and-shoulders pictures can be tricky unless you are able to use a long-focus lens, and so fill the picture-area satisfactorily from a distance of about 5 to 6 feet. Getting closer than this brings the risk of a subtle form of distortion, especially if the person has prominent features. With the 'standard' lens (the term usually given to that fitted to the average camera) it is generally safer therefore to content yourself with three-quarter length and full length studies of people.

Remember that bright sunshine is not the best lighting for outdoor portraits. It produces hard shadows and causes people to frown and screw up their faces. On such a day it is better to seek the shadow of a building; trees are only suitable if their foliage is really dense, otherwise they are inclined to give a dappled effect on the face, because the sunshine is filtered through the leaf spaces. If too close, leaves may also reflect their colour and so tint flesh-tones greenish. Soft sunshine, filtered through thin white cloud is naturally diffused, and will give good modelling without hard shadows.

Backgrounds

Avoid the 'fussy' kind of background that is full of intricate and distracting detail whenever you can—if you are after a portrait, as opposed to a shot of someone in a particular setting or location —a little extra care in choosing the right spot can make all the difference. If you're photographing in the garden, watch out for things like trellis, wire-netting, stray lengths of growth from nearby plants.

An old dodge is to stand your subject at an open doorway, or to utilize an open window; a plain or rough-cast wall can be effective, but *never* use one of ordinary brick. Sky backgrounds are popular. These generally mean working from a low viewpoint, and it isn't always easy to exclude unwanted objects such as poles, wires etc. Blossom and flower settings are very becoming for ladies; the light reflected from blossom can be very helpful in lessening shadow contrast, watch out though for reflected colour in the case of flowers.

The worst possible position your subject can take up is that when the shoulders are full square to the camera. Even when it is to be a full-face study, always have shoulders turned so that one is nearer than the other, the person then turning the head to look into the lens or any other direction indicated. There must be no evidence of posing or tenseness in the photograph, and the job cannot be done in five minutes. Half the battle is in getting, and keeping, the subject at ease; if you want a smile, your conversation should create one, not command it.

A gate can prove useful as something for the person to grasp, possibly lean over with or without hands on chin, a log or stile to sit on (or, in the case of a man, to put a foot on, in comfortable easy stance). The bank of a river or pool etc., is suitable, always providing you remember that it is the *person* you are out to photograph, not the setting. Regard the setting as an adjunct to the picture—a very necessary one—don't include too much of it, or it will compete for interest with the figure. It the subject wears spectacles, take care that they do not reflect the light and so obscure the eyes. A slight turn of the head, this way and that, a slight forward or backward tilt, will generally eliminate the trouble.

• • •

DO'S AND DONT'S FOR SPRINGTIME PHOTOGRAPHY

DO remember that blossom pictures *must* be sharp; unsharp blossom can look like cotton-wool. So focus accurately, see that depth-of-field is adequate, and use shutter speeds fast enough to overcome movement by breezes.

DON'T overlook your local parks when searching for spring subjects, but avoid the too-conventional flowerbed or layout (keep out those assertive name-tags and labels too, if you can!).

DO remember that flat lighting produces flat pictures. The spring scene always looks best in sunshine, even if this is not strong.

DON'T cram your pictures with a lot of unneccessary detail which has no bearing on the subject. Bold, simple treatment always scores.

DO use an exposure meter or some form of reliable exposure guide. Lighting can change very quickly in springtime, and strong contrasts are more often the rule than the exception, especially after a shower.

DON'T have woodland paths or country lanes running across *your picture area, dividing the composition into two parts. Choose viewpoints that show them going* into *the scene beyond.*

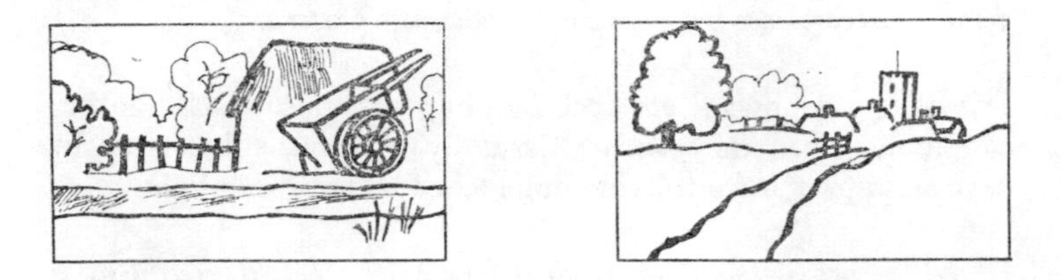

DO get in close for impact and texture. The delicate detail of flowers, newly-opening buds, blossom etc. cannot be captured from distant viewpoints; a long-focus lens can be a great help in many instances.

DON'T forget that outdoor subjects change and grow with such rapidity that it just doesn't do to put off photographing anything until the last moment. That last moment is often too late; a few showers, an extra burst of sunshine, and the face of the countryside has changed.

DO watch out for spectacular skies and interesting cloud formations; the shafts of sunshine which pierce through stormy banks of cumulus to spotlight buildings, trees, church towers etc. In open and semi-open landscape studies, these phenomena can be most impressive.

DON'T try 'stunty' viewpoints and tricks with country subjects; reserve them for unusual lighting etc. in town scenes. When including figures, make sure they are not out-of-character or unsuitably dressed.

DO watch that background; keep it plain and contrasting with the subject-proper whenever possible. Fussy, irritating highlights coming through hedges can spoil the best spring subject. Blue sky makes the best background for blossom; clouds so often merge into the subject's outlines.

DON'T ignore the 'pattern picture'. Spring sunshine, with its low-angle lighting, creates long shadows that are sometimes more interesting pictorially than the objects which cast them. Intricate 'bitty' detail however, does not necessarily constitute pattern.

DO take advantage of back-lighting and near-back-lighting conditions when they occur. Carefully exposed, subjects so lit have an impact and attraction unmatched by any other lighting.

DON'T work without an efficient lens hood, even if your lens is coated. One which completely encircles the lens is best; the 'sky shade' types which shield it from top-light only, are unsuitable whenever there is water in the foreground—because this can then reflect light upwards.

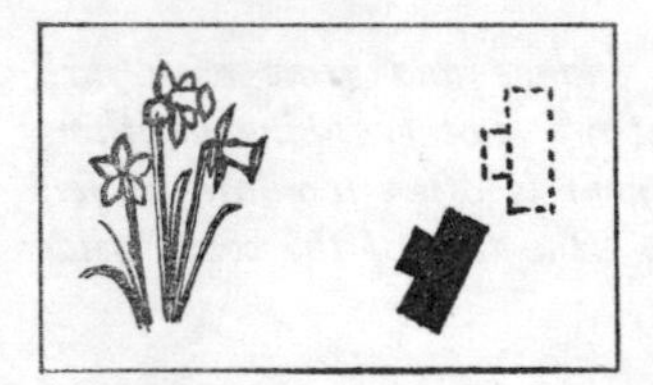

DO choose low viewpoints for small subjects near ground level. Whenever conditions permit, work with a tripod and compose your picture *leisurely*; don't be misled or over-influenced by colour alone.

DON'T try to get everything *sharp in your landscape studies, otherwise the feeling of distance and recession will be lost. Generally speaking, the foreground should be sharply recorded, unless you are after some special effect.*

DO be patient if you're photographing lambs, chicks or young animals; once you have frightened them, your chances of success are considerably lessened.

DON'T have 'half-way horizons' in landscape scenes. If the sky is the more interesting, let it occupy two-thirds of the frame, and vice-versa. Avoid 'plain' and empty foregrounds.

DO remember that the light and dark masses in any picture should be unequal. Regular, even disposition of shadow (except in pattern pictures) tends to create monotony and make the subject too 'ordinary'.

DON'T forget that if you wish to increase colour brightness (saturation) in a subject, give slightly less than normal exposure. Conversely, to quieten intense colours, slightly over-expose—but on no account overdo things.

● ● ●

PICTURES IN SUMMER

MORE COLOUR FILMS are exposed during summer than at any other time, chiefly of course, because it is the holiday season. However, it can bring photographic disappointments even on the brightest days, and frustration on dull and wet ones! Much of this is due to the prevailing *lighting*; the true pictorialist will despair the lack of low-angle, dramatic sunshine, or the softer atmosphere associated with other seasons. Nevertheless, there are still opportunities for interesting, unusual and worthwhile pictures, if one is prepared to be a little more observant.

Except in the early morning and late afternoon, the sun is too high overhead, producing those short downward shadows mentioned previously, so more reliance has to be placed on the colour-content and general interest of the subject itself. In the countryside, foliage has thickened and is less fresh and attractive; heat haze reduces visibility for distant views. By way of compensation there are sometimes sporadic thunderstorms which can give brooding, striking skies.

Subjects in town

In the hot, dusty streets, human-interest pictures are easier to get because the pace is slower. Even shutter speeds as slow as 1/30 sec. can capture groups lounging or chatting; take advantage of awnings and shop doorways to get back-lit shots with bold foregrounds—colourful sunblinds can often prove useful, too.

If depth-of-field (zone of sharpness for a given lens aperture and distance-setting) is at times insufficient to keep both subject and foreground sharply rendered, concentrate on your *subject*, but bear in mind that bright saturated colours can be irritating to the eye when out-of-focus. Rear views of people are sometimes more interesting than orthodox shots. Market stalls offer wonderful scope for 'candid' pictures; zone-focusing technique (as described in your camera instruction booklet) lends itself to this catch-as-catch-can type of photography, where it is essential to keep the camera as unobtrusive as possible. In this field the miniature scores, and its interchangeable lenses can be invaluable. Half-frames and sub-miniatures are also particularly suitable for such shots.

When your subjects include children, it is wise to work at faster shutter speeds, because of their unpredictable movements, and they are harder to catch unawares. Exposures must be calculated on a general basis; if you try to take a reading each time, you may miss lively expressions. Get in close with your camera if you can.

There are action shots to be had in parks and recreation grounds, where organized events are regular summer features. If you visit the swimming pool it is advisable to use an ultra-violet (U.V.) filter on your lens to counteract possible blueness reflected on skin tones. A high diver, poised to take off, can make a more satisfying subject than one actually diving. As with seaside shots, the main difficulty is in trying to isolate your subject from a crowded background, and it pays to work from low or high viewpoints rather than keep the camera at normal level. Don't concentrate on adults all the while—there's lots of fun going on among the youngsters at the shallow end!

Picturesque old streets and buildings are rewarding colour subjects, and if you can pick a spot where they lead towards a church tower, some imposing structure or tall trees for a background, you have the material for an attractive picture. There is usually a 'best' side of a street, dependent upon the positioning and character of the various buildings, their sizes, and the shadows they cast. On a bright day the difference between the light on one side and that on the other may be more than the contrast range of your film, and you will have to choose a viewpoint which includes a good deal less shadow, or take your pictures at some other time.

To wait until a street is relatively empty may give the scene a dead appearance; try to shoot when there is a pleasing balance with cars and people in acceptable positions. While a shutter speed of 1/100 sec. may be adequate to prevent blur with pedestrians, 1/250 sec. is safer for traffic.

In the country

Partly due to atmospheric haze, and partly due to the even spread of light, distant landscape as a pictorial subject is often disappointing; after a shower, visibility is better. Unless there is something or someone in the foreground, the effect of distance will be lost; once again, a U.V. or skylight filter can be helpful for reducing blueness. On cloudless days it is a good plan to try and break the monotonous sky tone by selecting a viewpoint that introduces foreground foliage or branches—this provides that needed foreground balance as well.

Undulating fields and country lanes are splendid subjects in soft evening light; so are village streets and thatched or oddly-shaped cottages. Rough walls and aged timbers have their textures revealed; but remember that the light is likely to tinge everything yellow, including the faces of anyone you may photograph. Don't dismiss the sunset picture as hackneyed and corny; maybe it is, but no two sunsets are alike, and a country setting makes a change from the frequently adopted water foregrounds. It is usually best to adjust your exposures so as to keep fairly rich colouring in the sky, leaving skyline and foreground as dark silhouettes. Never over-expose for this subject. September is a noted month for sunsets, especially in low-lying districts which can add eerie ground mists.

If you try your hand at photographing rainbows, slight *under-exposure* is recommended—the colours are by no means as strong as they appear to the eye. Overhead summer sunshine is hopeless for woodland studies, it scatters bitty, dappled specks everywhere besides making contrasts too high. At the best of times forest and woodland scenes can be tricky. There must be some 'way through' for the eye, otherwise it looks an impenetrable mass of trees. So avoid thickets, keep to the clearings and the outskirts. See that trunks in the background do not line up exactly with the edges of those in front, and avoid evenly spaced trees. A footpath, no matter how small, will lead your eye into the picture, a foreground fence or hedge will shut it out.

At the coast

Don't disbelieve the high readings your exposure meter gives when you are photographing at or near the coast, even on dull days it is always considerably lighter than it is inland. If you have loaded up with fairly fast colour film you may find that you need a neutral density filter to reduce the intensity of the light by a fixed ratio without affecting the colour balance. Without one, you might have to stop down your lens much more than you wish, and work at the fastest shutter speeds in order to prevent over-exposure; with the more modest type of camera, its fastest shutter speed might not be fast enough even when you have closed the lens aperture to its smallest stop. The situation is less likely to arise with slow or medium-speed films.

Swim-suit girls are always popular subjects, and offer an excellent chance for you to exercise your portrait technique, with either full-length, three-quarters (and head-and-shoulders if you have a long-focus lens) or close-up poses. A colourful beachball, raft or rubber animal can help the mood of the picture. Poses against a skyline of sand dunes or open sea still make attractive shots. Take great care of your equipment on the beach, and protect it from sand particles and salt spray by keeping everything (yes—the ever-ready case as well!) in a polythene bag; never leave it lying in full sunshine, whether it is loaded with film or not.

Ships and boats make most pleasing colour studies. The gay hues of the smaller craft will keep you busy selecting and grouping them to best advantage in your picture area. There is often a strong temptation to include too many, or too much of one;

this must be firmly resisted. The old cliche 'The part is greater than the whole' is invariably a safe yard-stick when in doubt; moored boats can so easily look a jumble if you take the lot. Sailing craft convey far less sense of movement when they are upright than when heeling over; you'll probably have to go to the end of the pier to get satisfactory pictures of them.

While you're on the pier, keep an eye open for possible 'candid' and human-interest shots, and as you approach the entrance once more, take advantage of the high viewpoint to get angle pictures of people on the beach immediately below. In the same vein, don't overlook little pools and rivulets left by the outgoing tide. Put a supplementary lens on your camera (unless you can get close enough without one) and get close-ups of seaweed, shells and aged timbers that were once breakwaters; exploit the patterns of the ripple shapes moulded in the glistening sand, the imprint of feet, and cloud reflections in pools. These things which seem so commonplace at the time, become wonderfully effective colour slides although they are simple in theme.

Stalking the lone seagull can be a thankless—and fruitless—task, with never a worthwhile picture unless lighting *and* setting happen to be right. Successful shots of gulls depend on luck and patience, with a few tit-bits to lure your victims; a long-focus lens is a great asset. Where there are fishing boats there is often a swirling flurry of gulls; with a shutter speed of 1/500 sec. or faster, you can hardly help getting lots of them if you pick your spot.

Difficult subjects

Seascapes and coastline studies are worthwhile only if conditions and setting are suitable. Cliffs and rugged coasts are difficult to deal with. Unless you are in a boat or a small, sharply curving bay, the result is often a one-sided picture with nothing to balance the land masses. Waves dashing against rocks bring the risk of wet equipment, but a carefully chosen corner, with rocky edge and foreground, will make a better study than that vast coastline of rollers. You may hit on a good viewpoint only to find that small waves have taken over, and that you've just missed a beauty on the rock you had previously focused on! It's all in the luck of the game. Shutter speeds faster than 1/500 sec. will tend to freeze the movement of waves too much.

• • •

TIPS FOR BETTER HOLIDAY PICTURES

You may pride yourself on your equipment. We all do—but it's still a wise precaution to check everything before you set off. Avoid taking chances with worn parts, make sure the carrying strap of the ever-ready case and gadget bag are sound; constant bending of 'dry' leather causes cracking, and eventual breakage. If you are taking *new* equipment, familiarize yourself with it thoroughly first.

Take a 'write-on-anything' black pencil with you (such as Koh-I-Noor '*Allwrite*' 1555). *This will enable you to number and/or make notes on metal cassette containers, film leaders etc. without the slightest trouble, and serve as an emergency 'toucher-upper' should you inadvertently scratch the inner edge of your lenshood, causing bright metal to show.*

Before you go, think about the kind of pictures you hope to take, and the way you will try to take them. If you haven't been to that particular spot before, read up its attractions, and plan the sort of subjects you want—and those you wish to avoid. For instance, if it's by the sea, decide if you want to tackle beach shots of children, general views and rocks and so on. It's been done before —now try to think how your shots will be different. A map or guide can be a great time-saver, and will give you some idea of what to expect; the *Photographer' Maps* issued by Kodak's are very helpful.

Your own children playing on the beach may be your main target, but keep an eye on other people's children too. Get down to their level; shoot while they are busy—not *while they look at your lens. Introduce an animal, and your picture-recipe is a cinch.*

No matter how attractive the scene and your surroundings, the part is still usually better than the whole. One 'take-in-everything' shot is sufficient to remind you of a district; after that, concentrate on *selective* picture-making, including close-ups where possible.

Unless your tripod is a massive affair, take it with you; strap it on the outside of your luggage if you like. That attractive view you find late in the evening (or sunsets) won't suffer from camera shake, and you'll get needle-sharp pictures when you use a long-focus lens. For interior studies of old churches, buildings, etc. a tripod is a must.

An emergency 'changing bag' can be made by setting up the tripod (without extending the legs) on newspaper spread on a

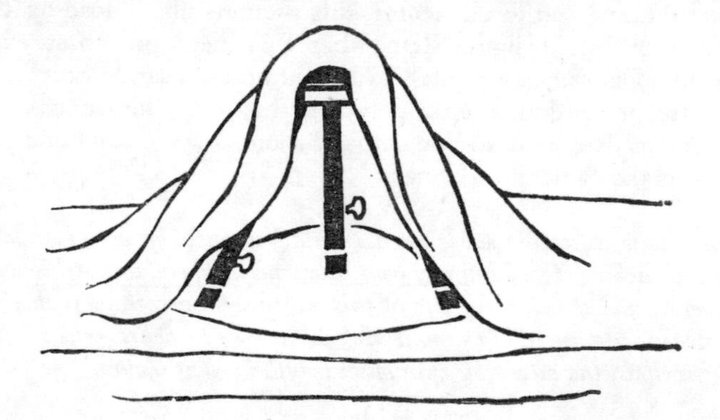

bed, covering it completely with the bed-clothes to form a light-proof tent for loading cassettes, releasing jammed film etc. A companion should help by tucking the bedclothes securely round your arms before you commence 'darkroom operations'. This is useful if the film comes away from the cassette in your camera, and no convenient cupboard is available while you are on holiday.

A country holiday suggests leafy lanes and woodland subjects. You won't like your results if the sun is overhead or harsh. The first condition gives bitty, dappled overall shadows, while harsh lighting will 'kill' any woodland study. Early morning and evening are the best times during the summer months; slight mist can be providential—but not for open views.

Exceptional subjects are always worth several exposures, made at varying angles and viewpoints—and frequently distance and exposure times too. A second visit in different lighting conditions is also sometimes worthwhile.

Shoot a few signs and signposts from time to time—they make excellent 'titles' to mix in with your slides, and help the audience to pinpoint the localities you show them.

Everyone knows the elementary instructions about loading the camera in bright light. Remember that near the coast even shaded spots can be bright. Never load up on a sandy beach. As an extra precaution, keep a polythene bag over the camera and its ever-ready case until you actually shoot. Regard sand and salt spray as the camera's enemies.

If you take a flexible cable release (and you should), avoid kinking it when packing, Once sharply bent, the inner cable seldom straightens properly, and the working life of this most useful accessory is thereby shortened. Again, don't 'make do' with a very short release; for effectiveness, the advisable minimum length is eight inches.

Unless you have already done so, insure all your photographic equipment. In the event of theft, damage or loss, the serial numbers and other identification of cameras and lenses will be needed—so make sure you have a copy of these details with you.

It is possible to burn a hole in a cloth focal-plane shutter if the camera is left facing the sun, with the lens focused at infinity, whereupon it becomes a much-too-efficient 'burning glass'. Similarly it can 'hot-up' metal focal-plane shutters unless due care is taken.

Waterfalls—so attractive as a subject—are notoriously difficult to photograph satisfactorily. Too fast a shutter speed (1/1000 sec. for instance) 'freezes' the movement, tending to give an unnatural appearance; too slow a speed allows blur and smoothes out the ripples. Take more than one shot, varying your shutter speeds from 1/500 to 1/250 sec. according to your distance from the water, and its speed of movement. The same advice applies to shots of waves—which should never be shot 'square-on'.

Colour films dislike excessive heat. Never leave them in your car if it is parked in the sun, or lying around in a hot spot. Humid conditions can produce colour casts or fungus growths. Try to avoid marked temperature changes; store films in metal containers (or wrap in foil) with a little desiccant such as silica gel *to protect them against moisture, when visiting hot climates.*

When photographing landscapes and general scenes, watch out for scraps of paper, cigarette cartons etc. littering the foreground. It is the work of a moment to pick them up before you shoot. Many otherwise excellent pictures have been spoilt through unnoticed litter; you can do nothing about removing such objects from a tiny transparency; but how large they look on the screen!

If your camera has no film-type reminder disc incorporated, you may like to put a piece of adhesive tape on the back of the ever-ready case, bearing a slip of paper with the loaded film details written with a ball-pen. By using surgical (opaque) tape instead, the details can be written directly on to the tape surface. Any sticky deposit remaining after removal can be cleaned off with spirit.

There is always argument as to whether a figure should be included in a purely pictorial landscape or not. The important thing however, is that if a person *is* included, then he or she must be in character with the setting. Country clothing goes with country scenes.

When you cannot decide whether a subject fits an 'upright' shape better than a horizontal or vice versa, take one of each (unless your camera has a square format). Don't make a habit of this, though, or you may find your ability to 'see' a composition gradually declining!

When you buy a cassette of 35 mm. film, it often happens that the leader strip has a definite fold or kink in it just where it emerges from the cassette mouth. It is always advisable to straighten this out by bending it in the opposite direction; neglecting to do so can sometimes result in faulty take-up, the perforations either missing the camera sprockets or engaging them at an angle. The straightening-out process must be accurately carried out, otherwise you may get *two* kinks to contend with, instead of one.

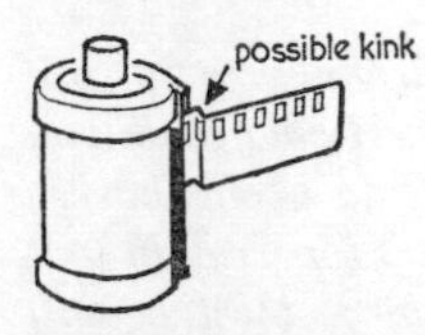

Study the local viewcards, and thus find the recognized beauty-spots. Much-photographed as they may have been, there is usually a worthwhile shot or two to be had from them, preferably from different viewpoints. Should the weather make photography virtually impossible, you might like to buy a few as a record. Alternatively, those same cards could show you the places you want to (photographically) avoid.

When tall buildings, spires etc. make tilting the camera unavoidable, go the whole hog and tilt strongly from a closer viewpoint. Slight tilting can be irritating on the screen; intentional diagonals caused by strong tilting often help to convey height better. Using a wide-angle lens will probably overcome the problem, but render the subject less imposing.

Keep a note of the things and places you photograph. Thirty-six exposures go quickly when you're on holiday (and twelve or eight even quicker)!; so pencil a number on the film leader or backing paper when you unload. Repeat this number against the list of subjects on that film—even if you do have a good memory.

It is often worthwhile to pack a flash unit—it may be the means of securing many a difficult shot. Today's gear is light and compact, and can be carried without undue hardship. The intensity of summer sunshine frequently creates harsh shadows which detract from otherwise successful colour pictures; used as a fill-in to lighten these dark areas, even the smallest flash unit becomes invaluable.

Interiors are often better photographed without sunshine, so the dull days you get may be turned to good advantage. Sunshine streaming through windows creates contrasts with which many colour films cannot cope (especially the slower kinds of film).
Flower studies of the richer, deeper blooms are frequently improved by sunless conditions too, and shots of colourful gardens, sea-front ornamental beds etc. can become dull-day subjects. Soft, hazy sunshine however, is often ideal—and for portraits as well.

Many people like to squeeze in an 'extra' exposure or two at either end of a film. It frequently pays off—but sometimes those extra frames are punched or marked during processing; therefore, don't take important subjects on 'bonus' frames!

Don't get flustered if you have to work quickly to capture some passing action. Forget your meter for the first shot, then *follow your usual routine regarding exposure etc.—if there's time.*

On the beach, it pays to keep a ready trigger-finger and use 'zone-focusing' technique. Human-interest is not static; make 1/125 sec. your slowest shutter speed if you can. A pre-set camera often makes all the difference between success and failure.

Any bright red object in a scene photographed in colour automatically becomes the focal point for the eye when viewing. A touch of red suitably placed in a 'quiet' subject can 'make' the picture; in the wrong spot, can spoil it.

If you have any trouble with your equipment while you're away, don't go prodding and pushing, trying to fix things for yourself. See a local dealer immediately.

When circumstances necessitate the use of the slower shutter speeds, and you have no tripod or handy support for the camera, the following trick can be most helpful: take up the slack of your camera strap or neck sling by winding it round one hand, so that it is pulled taut aginst the back of your neck when holding the camera up to your eye. Grip both camera and strap firmly, and with the instrument thus 'tied to your face' as it were, you stand a much better chance of avoiding shake; some can even hold it steady at shutter speeds of 1/10*th or* 1/8*th second in this way.*

Carry a short length of string in your pocket, together with a couple of paper clips and elastic bands. If you knot the string at one-foot intervals it will serve as a convenient measure for close-ups, it can also be used to tie round the feet of the tripod to prevent slipping on smooth surfaces, or to tie back unwanted sprays when photographing blossom etc. The paper clips will hold a sheet of newspaper on a hedge or bush to act as a reflector when needed, and the elastic bands will secure any exposed roll film that has lost its sticker. Other uses for these items will probably suggest themselves.

To gain extra height when a high viewpoint is called for, the camera can be held above the head and directed towards the subject; reflex cameras make it possible to view and focus from this position, otherwise focusing must be pre-set. The technique is invaluable when photographing sporting, carnival events etc. surrounded by people —aiming the camera is then a matter of judgment. Shutter speeds slower than 1/100*th or* 1/125*th second are inadvisable because of the possibility of camera movement.*

Low viewpoints make a subject look taller. When photographing people in this way, a too-close approach may produce heavy modelling of the lower limbs.

• • •

HINTS ON CLOSE-UPS

CLOSE-UP STUDIES OF relatively small objects are among the most striking—and fascinating—subjects for reversal colour photography, bringing texture and detail to the screen in a way that no other medium can. Most cameras have distances around 3½ to 3 feet as their nearest focusing points, but you can easily get closer to things merely by fitting a suitable supplementary or close-up lens over the camera lens. Some makers supply special ones for their particular cameras, others are usually available to fit lens mounts of various diameters.

You can choose from three powers: a +1 lens which has a focal length of 1 metre (39 inches), a +2 lens with a focal length of ½ metre, and +3 of ⅓ metre. With your camera set to infinity, a close-up lens focuses sharply on an object at a distance equal to its focal length; this distance is reduced as you change your camera lens focusing to its setting of 3 feet. The ranges covered by the three supplementary lenses are shown in this table:

Camera lens setting	+1 power	+2 power	+3 power
At infinity	39 ins.	19½ ins.	13 ins.
At 3 feet	19 ins.	12½ ins.	9½ ins.

The snags? There are two: because depth-of-field is very limited at these close distances, you have to stop down the lens to a small aperture (as small as the exposure time permits, preferably *f*/11 or smaller); and the problem of parallax. This latter trouble arises because unless the camera is a single-lens reflex, the viewfinder no longer shows the area covered by the lens. If it is positioned immediately above the lens, it becomes a question of tilting the camera upwards so that no 'cut-off' occurs. The amount of tilt (or raising of camera) increases as you get closer to the subject.

Parallax correction

As a rough working guide to the amount of tilt or lift required to overcome this difference in what the lens sees and what the viewfinder sees: with a +1 lens about one-eighth of the top of the picture will be cut off if the camera is not tilted; $\frac{1}{6}$ with a +2 lens, and approximately $\frac{1}{4}$ with a +3 lens. It follows that if after sighting your subject in the ordinary way, you tilt or raise the camera so that what you see in the viewfinder 'drops' to correspond with these amounts (according to the power of the supplementary lens you fit), the camera lens is then covering the area you originally sighted. However, test exposures should be made (using black-and-white film for economy if you wish), as each camera varies in this matter.

The above procedure applies when the camera is used for 'horizontal' shape pictures; turned for the 'upright' shape, the viewfinder then becomes positioned at the *side* of the lens, and it is necessary to turn or move the camera a little to one side instead of raising it. Difficulties arise if the viewfinder is not set centrally above the lens in the camera body; one must then try to 'aim' the lens by imagining a line running through the centre of it, towards the centre of the subject. In other words, it is usually better to disregard the viewfinder entirely.

Some camera manufacturers supply a little 'framing' device

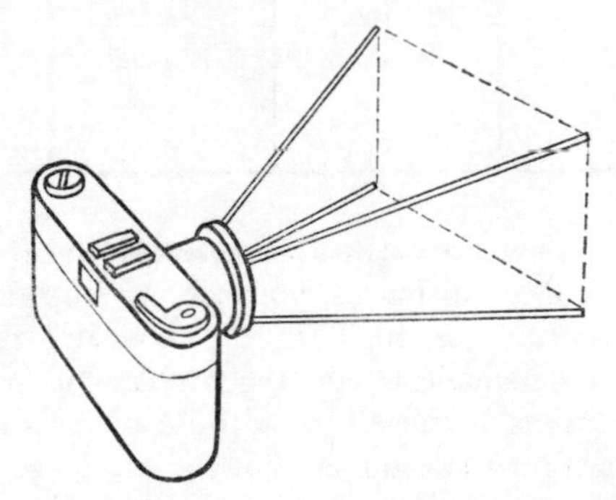

which extends in front of the lens, and indicates the area covered, and the taking-distance. Supplementary lenses for twin-lens reflex cameras are sold in matched pairs, so that one can focus and view as in the ordinary way. In addition, parallax-correcting lenses are made for the 'Rollei' cameras.

Measuring distances

In some instances, the tables accompanying the close-up lenses give working distances (subject-to-camera) which must be measured from the *focal plane* (i.e., where the film runs through the camera 'gate' behind the lens); but generally, the required distances are measured from the front of the close-up lens—a flexible steel tape measure is convenient for this. Remember, that because of the shallow depth-of-field, you cannot merely *guess;* accurate measurement is essential. When using close-up lenses, no exposure increase is needed. With very small subjects, reflected light readings can be difficult and unreliable; allowance must be made for background influence on the meter cell whenever it differs strongly from the subject in lighting or colour. Many prefer to take incident light readings, modifying the results by increasing exposures ½ to 1 stop for dark subjects, and reducing by ½ stop for light subjects.

Cameras that take interchangeable lenses can increase their focusing range by means of extension tubes or bellows attachments. This involves exposure increases, because as the camera lens itself is extended, the nominal *f/* values engraved on it no longer apply. Details and exposure factors are supplied with the tubes and bellows. The following table is typical:

EXPOSURE FACTORS FOR LENS EXTENSIONS

Scale of reproduction	Exposure factor (increase required)
1:4	x 1½
1:3	x 1¾
1:2	x 2
1:1	x 4

Cameras with built-in meters run into trouble with close-ups, in that once set up in position, the meter cannot be used properly; so readings must be taken *first.*

It goes without saying, that the camera should be on a sturdy shake-free tripod or support, and the shutter released by means of a flexible cable release.

Usually it pays to direct light into the shadow areas with a reflector; a white card or cloth supported at a suitable angle will

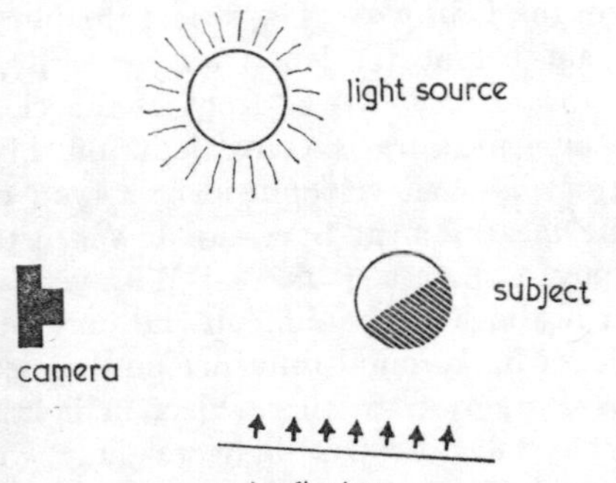

prove adequate. As the subject area is small, this is seldom difficult to arrange. To rely solely on *one* exposure is unwise; experts frequently take three or more shots in such circumstances, varying the exposures either way from that indicated by the meter.

Close-ups taken on dull days are often more successful if flash is used, the exposure being calculated as though flash were the sole light source. This treatment causes the background to appear darkened, and is effective when photographing flowers. Single specimens, small objects etc. can be photographed against a matt black card background, either by daylight alone, or with the addition of flash if desired.

Summing up: Use a small lens aperture, focus accurately to measured distances, make due allowance for parallax when 'aiming' the camera, avoid camera-shake.

• • •

TIPS ON TAKING FLOWERS

SIMPLY LOADING YOUR camera with colour film and firing away at the brightest flowers you can find is *not* the way to success. Unless your instrument is capable of focusing to 3 or 3½ feet—or of accepting either supplementary or long-focus lenses—it is better to content yourself with 'open' shots of flower beds, borders and so on, concentrating on general appeal instead of trying to capture intricate detail. This is the easiest form of flower-photography, and can be indulged in whenever there is access to displays, such as in public parks and gardens. The problem is to select them judiciously.

Flowers have texture as well as shape and colour, and this is best revealed by lighting coming from one side, (i.e. side-lighting) with the sun lightly veiled by the thinnest of white clouds. Oddly enough, some which have yellow-green leaves sometimes photograph better in sunless or near-sunless conditions; study their appearance as the sun comes and goes, and you can decide this for yourself. Normally however, dull days make flower subjects less inviting. There is always a temptation to 'get in as many as you can'—to present a great carpet of blooms that can so easily become merely colour for colour's sake. Masses and groupings covering *smaller* areas have considerable appeal; indeed, massed blooms photograph better than straggling clumps or narrow borders.

For tall flowers such as hollyhocks and sunflowers, the best background is a blue sky; beware of deep blue skies as backgrounds for blue and mauve-blue flowers, or those vivid red and orange—the visual impact can jar and irritate! Many of the quieter-hued flowers, those of subtle delicate colourings, generally make the most effective studies. Almost invariably, a plain background is the most suitable, although in practice it is usually hard to find, and it should contrast well with the subject. This latter condition is generally achieved when back-lighting creates deep shadows.

Shutter speeds must be fast enough to cope with any movement caused by the breeze (and even on a 'calm' day there is a risk of some movement at times); at a distance of 6ft. or more 1/50 or 1/60 sec. are the slowest advisable. Small flowers need low viewpoints and a close approach. Make sure that any dead flowers, unwanted sprays etc. are first removed, and tidy up the background. Extra care at this stage makes all the difference! Flat lighting should be avoided, since shadows are needed to create form and texture. Forward-thrusting flowers can be difficult to contain within the depth-of-field for adequate sharpness, it is then better to fasten them back unobtrusively or remove them altogether. Some photographers 'cheat' a little by adding another bloom here and there to fill awkward gaps and improve the arrangement. If you've a mind to do this, see to it that the effect is entirely natural in appearance—it is all too easy to overdo things.

Indoors

Photographing flowers indoors requires both technical skill and a flair for grouping and arranging. Even the loveliest of blooms can be ineffective if the setting and arrangements are not tasteful; any attempt at 'stunty' set-ups is likely to ruin everything. Quite often the best result is achieved by standing the flowers on a window-ledge (not in direct sunshine) and using a white reflector on the shadow side. If the light falls from above and to one side, all should be well.

The vase or container should be plain, or relatively so, and in keeping with the kind of flower; large blooms need substantial vases, dainty flowers need delicate ones. Small flowers require a true close-up technique. For ease of handling, they may be held in position by 'Plasticine'; remember though, that they quickly wilt. The grouping should be kept almost within one plane, and the lens stopped down as much as possible, otherwise depth-of-field may be insufficient.

• • •

PHOTOGRAPHING BY ARTIFICIAL LIGHT

PERHAPS THE GREATEST advantage offered by artificial light photography is that of the *control* it permits, especially in the case of portraiture. In daylight, the direction, power, and kind of light are determined by prevailing conditions; but when working solely with artificial light, the lamp(s) may be placed to produce any desired effect or balance, and lighting adjusted to suit the subject—instead of the other way round. An impressive array of lamps and lighting equipment does *not* necessarily guarantee the finest results. While it is true that a greater range of effects is possible with, say, three lamps than with two, it does not follow that six or eight lamps would be even better!

For informal home shooting, you can of course make do with the ordinary household lighting fixtures if you remove the shades and replace the lamps with No. 1 photoflood lamps; but the position of the ceiling light is too high, giving those overhead, downward shadows we were at pains to avoid in summer sunshine. Furthermore, photofloods are meant to be used in metal reflectors, and telescopic stands complete with swivelling reflectors are not expensive items. The domestic lighting circuit will safely take up to three No. 1 photofloods (rated 275 watts, running life approximately three hours).

Exposure

A photo-electric meter is preferable for exposure determination; some workers use the incident light method, other stick to conventional reflected light readings. By taking into account the inverse square law of illumination however (the light from a lamp falling off as the square of its distance), a system of 'guide numbers' can be adopted. Moving a lamp *twice* its distance from the subject involves multiplying the exposure by *four*, not merely doubling it. Remember that you should not mix photoflood lighting with daylight, nor with ordinary domestic lighting.

Quite a lot can be accomplished by using only two lamps, and for negative-colour film a simple arrangement is to have both the same distance from the subject, and at about a 45° angle, but with one lamp slightly higher than the other. The best way to arrange any lighting set-up is to start by placing your main lamp carefully, then move the other(s) into position, noting the effect created. The second (fill-in) lamp should be about 1½ times the distance of the main lamp. and slightly lower in height; increasing this distance increases the contrast ratio. Quite small adjustments in height, angle and distance can make an appreciable difference—and remember that a cast shadow appears much less dark to the eye than it will record on the film. The following table will give you some idea as to what exposure times are likely to be, using two No. 1 photofloods in an average-sized room with light-coloured walls.

LAMPS-TO-SUBJECT EXPOSURE GUIDE

Film speed (tungsten) ASA	*Shutter speed sec.*	*Lamps-to-subject distance in feet (Two lamps i.e. main light and fill-in)*				
		3	4½	6	9	12
40	1/15	*f*/9	*f*/6.3	*f*/4.5	*f*/3.2	*f*/2.3
80	1/30	*f*/9	*f*/6.3	*f*/4.5	*f*/3.2	*f*/2.3
100	1/60	*f*/11	*f*/8	*f*/5.6	*f*/4	*f*/2.8

The figures are approximate, and are based on the use of two lamps in satin-finish aluminium reflectors, both illuminating the same area. To reduce shadows on background, an extra lamp may be directed onto it without substantially affecting the exposure.

If you intend to do much artificial light photography, a foot switch that will control up to three lamps is a good investment. The limiting size of the average living room makes true portraiture difficult, but not impossible if you remember to make sure that neither camera nor background are too close to the subject. A flat-painted wall is an excellent background; a light one can be made to appear darker simply by restricting the amount of light reaching it. Coloured walls at the sides can reflect their colouring onto the person's flesh tones if at all near.

For safe working, it is a good plan to have the camera lens approximately level with the subject's eyes, and that means getting down to it when you're photographing children on the floor. Avoid low viewpoints for people with heavy chins or neck-lines, avoid high ones for people who are thin-on-top or who have broad foreheads, avoid profile shots of anyone with prominent features.

Outdoors

Perhaps the most interesting thing about night photography outdoors, is that scenes and objects which are quite ordinary by day, take on altogether new interest and pictorial value as night falls. It doesn't really matter which type of colour film you load up with, since neither artificial light nor daylight type are balanced for the various kinds of lighting encountered; many prefer the rendering given by daylight film. However, in view of the nature of the subject, there is little point in increasing your difficulties by working with slow films; medium-speed or fast ones will give plenty of scope as a rule, although high-speed films are obviously better whenever people or slow-moving vehicles are to be included.

If you wait until it actually *is* dark, the colour film will give you dense black backgrounds without detail, the bright lights becoming isolated and without any visible means of support. The trick is to keep the subject more within the limitations of the film by making your exposures at *dusk*, when the remaining daylight helps to reduce the contrast between highlights and shadows. The results will still look like night photographs, but outlines and main detail will be preserved. Again, shooting at this time allows shorter exposure times, and quite a bit can be done without a tripod (using medium-speed film, a typical exposure at dusk could be in the region of 1/30 sec. at *f*/2.8). Much depends upon the sort of effect you want—a longer exposure will record the visual appearance of the buildings and lessen the brilliance of the lights, and vice versa. If your meter is sensitive enough to give you a reading in the ordinary way, it will probably pay you to stop down the lens one stop (or even two) lower than that indicated, for a more convincing night effect.

Never work without a lens hood. The direct rays of intense light near at hand are best avoided, or you might get flare patches. For static subjects it is best to use a sturdy tripod, not only to guard against possible camera shake, but also to allow the lens to be stopped down for greater depth-of-field, which is frequently desirable. Unless you cover the lens whenever vehicles enter the field of view, their lights will register a long winding trail across your picture. A companion can be a great help in many ways, and a small pocket torch is invaluable in enabling you to read lens settings quickly and easily.

EXPOSURE GUIDE FOR OUTDOOR NIGHT PICTURES

(Using 50 ASA film)

Subject	Suggested exposures			
	Speed	*f*/No.	Speed	*f*/No.
Illuminated signs, street lights etc. *at dusk*	1/30	2.8	1/15	2.8
Bright street lighting	1/15	2.8	1/8	2.8
Christmas lights (London)	1/8	2.8	1/15	2.8
Piccadilly Circus	1/30	3.5	1/30	2.8
Advertising signs (various colours)	1/30	4	1/30	2.8
Floodlit buildings (white light)	1 sec.	2.8	2 secs.	2.8
Floodlit buildings (coloured lights)	5 secs.	2.8	8 secs.	2.8
Shop windows	1/8	2.8	1/15	2.8
Shop windows (bright)	1/30	2.8	1/30	3.5
Sunsets (including sun)	1/60	4	1/60	2.8
Sunsets (sun behind clouds)	1/15	4	1/15	2.8

(Note: these exposure times are only approximate, and are intended to serve as a working basis. For 25 ASA films, the given times must be doubled. For close viewpoints, smaller lens apertures with appropriate exposure increases will give greater depth-of-field).

Daylight *or* artificial light type colour film may be used, as neither kind is balanced to deal with every sort of light source encountered.

Wet nights, with glistening pavements and road surfaces broken by interesting reflections, can often 'make' the picture. Shop windows are worthwhile subjects if you work from fairly close viewpoints at an angle. Fluorescent strip lighting needs daylight type film, preferably. Watch for *subtle* lighting and local detail, and remember that fog can give you striking effects near light sources. A few well-chosen slides of night scenes included with your usual ones will not only widen the appeal of your colour show, but also add contrast that will benefit daytime shots.

• • •

USING FLASH INDOORS

UNLIKE ANY OTHER form of lighting, flash does not allow *visual assessment* of any given lighting effect beforehand; in other words, one cannot see just how the subject will look with the light coming from certain angles until *after* the picture is taken. Again, the all-important adjustments for flash-to-subject distances that must be made periodically, can sometimes result in the loss of some brief interesting situation or expression when you are taking family pictures.

Fortunately, because of *colour differences* in such things as clothing, furnishings, etc., flash-on-camera can be quite successful with colour films, and for straightforward shots, the absence of modelling shadows is not disastrous. Provided that correct exposure has been given, many people are perfectly happy with flash-on-camera technique, and there is something to be said for the argument that this frontal lighting with its dark outline shadows immediately behind the subject, can often appear less 'heavy' than the larger spread of shadows created by lighting coming from an agle. Frontal flash also has the advantage that there are no trailing extension wires to get in the way and hamper movement.

In general, the secret of success lies largely in keeping the subject fairly 'shallow' whenever possible—a too-near foreground may otherwise burn out through over-exposure, and/or a too-distant background may appear too dark through under-exposure. It pays, therefore, to see that your family groups are not literally spread around the room; but don't go to the other extreme, and pack them close in unnatural positions.

Bounce flash

To eliminate the subtly characteristic effects of frontal flash, the adoption of 'bounce flash' is often recommended, whereby the flash is aimed at the ceiling and walls near to the subject, these reflecting the light in soft, non-directional fashion. But this too, has its snags; coloured walls reflect their own colouration and so can mar the faithfulness of flesh-tones, and exposure can no longer be directly based on the guide number system. By estimating the total distance of flash from ceiling, and ceiling from subject, then increasing the aperture given by this distance in conjunction with the guide number by 1½ to 2 more stops approximately accurate exposures should result. But some experiment is needed.

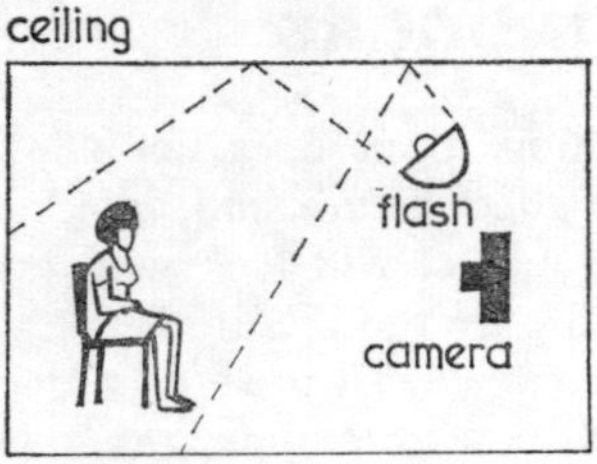

Having once found this 'bounce factor' it can be relied upon for any future shots made in that or similar rooms. For obvious reasons, bounce flash is more suitable for small and medium-sized rooms than for large ones, and because it gives softer effects, pictures so produced lack sparkle. It is usually best to position your subject near a corner of the room, or near a wall.

If you wish to use the flash well away from *the camera*, an extension lead is necessary. For a start, a placing that throws light on the subject at an angle of about 45° (above and to one side of the camera), should give pleasing results as long as you arrange for a suitable white reflector to be near the subject. This can consist of a white cloth or sheet supported so that it throws light into the shadows made by the flash. It is worthwhile getting someone to hold an ordinary domestic light bulb in the position the flashbulb is to occupy, to get some measure of guidance for (1) lighting the subject, (2) placing the white reflector, and (3) discovering surfaces and objects which would reflect the flash back into the lens. Unfortunately, although extended flash methods make for better portraiture, they do not lend themselves to photographing lively children, animals, or any non-static subject.

Bare-bulb flash

As a compromise between the shadow problems of direct flash and the softness of bounce flash, you may like to try *bare-bulb* flash. For this, the metal reflector of the flash unit must be removed, and the flash held (or positioned) well away from the camera. *Never use the bare bulb on or near the camera.* Since less light is now reaching the subject, an increase in exposure becomes necessary, and the lens should be opened up about two stops more.

This method gives softer shadows, containing more detail; and if you fix the flash on some sort of stand so that its distance from the subject is constant, you can change camera viewpoint and taking-distance without changing your exposure settings.

Electronic flash

Greater scope is offered by electronic flash because of its action-stopping ability. Although the light approximates to daylight, there is sometimes a tendency to blueness in transparencies, and a slightly 'warm' filter such as Wratten 81A can improve matters. Young children and animals are less likely to be scared by electronic flash than by flashbulbs, and its only drawback is that you cannot remove the reflector for bare-bulb shots. Whichever type of equipment or technique you favour, a little constructive thinking beforehand will pay dividends: *plan* your homely shots to *look* homely . . . and unplanned!

The everyday domestic scenes—children at play indoors, helping in the kitchen, in the bath or tucked up in bed—make rewarding subjects for colour if you set the scene in advance. Remove fussy and intruding objects such as ornaments, vases, etc; aim for simplicity. If you are taking straightforward interiors, try not to re-arrange the furniture too much or it will not be 'home' as you know it. Remember too, not to tilt the camera and thus get converging verticals. Watch out for tobacco smoke; even what may seem to the eye to be only a faint haze, can act like a fog when you're using flash, and give 'flat' images in the camera. The further the subject from the camera, the greater the effect of a

GUIDE NUMBERS FOR BLUE FLASHBULBS

(Daylight type reversal colour films)

Flashbulb	Shutter speed and synchronizing lever position 'X' or 'M'	Colour film speed				
		ASA 25–32 *BS* 25–26°	40–50 27–28°	64–80 29–30°	100–125 31–32°	160–200 33–34°
PF. 1B	1/25–1/30 sec. X	65	85	105	135	170
No. 1BS	1/100–1/125 sec. M	50	64	85	102	130
	1/200–1/250 sec. M	38	48	60	80	95

These guide numbers are approximate, and are based on the use of a satin-finish reflector on the flash unit, and for medium-sized rooms with light-coloured walls.

Note: The guide number is simply the product of the flash-to-subject distance and the *f*/number at which the lens is set.

smoky atmosphere. When you photograph people wearing spectacles, never let them look directly at the camera if the flash unit is mounted on it, or reflections may completely blot out their eyes in your picture.

• • •

DAYLIGHT INDOORS

ONE OF THE MAIN difficulties about photographing indoors by daylight is that in most rooms the light comes from one direction only, falling off very rapidly in intensity towards the other side of the room. If the sun is shining directly through the windows, the result in a transparency is likely to be just a small area in natural colour, with the rest in varying depths of 'heavy' colour and dark shadow—the effect being most marked when the slower types of colour films are used. But where windows are covered by net curtaining, the strong sunshine is then diffused and softened, permitting effective indoor shots.

Brightly lit windows themselves should not be included in the picture, because of the high contrast created between these and the rest of the interior. Such contrasts can be acceptably balanced by using the outdoor synchro-sun technique (fill-in flash) and/or 'bouncing' the flash off the ceiling. For indoor portraits by daylight alone, it is usually best to sit the subject three-quarter face towards the windows, and direct light into the shadowed side of the face by means of a white reflector such as a sheet or tablecloth.

The *kind* of daylight which comes through the windows must also be taken into account, otherwise results might easily have bluish tendencies. An ultra-violet (U.V.) or Skylight filter will help to correct this, and allow you to take pleasing shots even on overcast days. The exposure meter reading should be taken from the medium-tones of the subject for full-length (sitting) studies, and from the face for closer portraiture. Without a meter, correct exposure assessment is difficult, if not impossible to achieve; never point the meter cell towards the windows (unless you are using the incident light method) and remember to allow for reciprocity failure if exposures are lengthy.

In most cases a tripod will be needed; room lights should not be switched on, nor should photoflood lamps be used to raise the general level of lighting—daylight and artificial light should never be mixed. Sometimes an upstairs room will prove brighter, and there is often less bric-à-brac cluttering up the background. As with outdoor portraiture, the plainer the background, the better, unless you are after a 'homely' setting.

Once you have found a good position for your sitter in relation to the window(s), try the effect of changing the camera viewpoint, moving in an arc from the front to the side of the subject. Note the changes in modelling that this presents. As you move towards the centre of the room, more of the shadowed side of your sitter's face is shown. By raising or lowering the camera also, certain features can be subdued or emphasized. Your sitter must be prepared to move the head and shoulders slowly in any direction you indicate; a tilt here, a turn there, can make all the difference.

Other subjects

If you have a convex mirror available, attractive shots can be had by hanging it near the window so that it reflects the scene outside. Get close to it with your camera (3 to 3½ feet) otherwise the reflected images will appear unimportant; depth-of-field should preferably cover both the actual mirror in its frame and the scene it reflects. This means considerable stopping-down of the lens, focusing on the mirror itself will cause the reflected scene to be unsharp. A similar, yet better, effect will be obtained if you use a large silver witch-ball; its 'all-round' reflective capacity will take in the whole room, the camera—and you! For this reason, avoid having numerous light-sources.

When window panes are liberally splashed by large raindrops, why not try shooting the outside scene *through* a selected area, so 'framing' the view with water droplets? The most pleasing effect is usually created by keeping the raindrops sharply defined, while the view is somewhat out-of-focus.

● ● ●

COLOURFUL AUTUMN

AUTUMN IS A wonderful season for colour photographers; everywhere there is colour and spectacle. Nature is always riotous, and even the most unimaginative layman cannot help but be impressed by the autumn display. Unfortunately, it is all too easy to let such beauty go to one's head, to let it induce a 'trigger-happy' condition that urges one to shoot away happily at almost every pleasant scene in sight, especially when the sun is 'just right' and picture opportunities are limited. It is, of course, easy to preach, and yet so difficult to avoid succumbing to the temptation of capturing plenty of colour before winter takes over . . . just one more here, and one more there.

One of the main differences between the less-advanced photographer and the experienced, is that of restraint and discrimination in choice of subject and viewpoint. To take a technically-excellent photograph is one thing, to achieve a *picture* is another. Most colour workers will agree that some of their finest results have come from *simple* subjects and close-up studies. By taking pains not to allow the general impact of rich colouring to over-influence your judgment, greater success is likely.

The trick is to avoid *sameness*; and this is harder than it seems. Twenty colour slides of trees in autumn can be most gratifying; one hundred and twenty can bring boredom. It is not sufficient merely to photograph different kinds of leaves or vary the taking-angle and distance. Selective perception combined with careful technique is the only answer, unless you are content to let the colours speak for themselves.

As a rule, you will find the larger type of leaf (lime, horse chestnut, plane, beech etc) more rewarding than those of the smaller variety (birch, hornbeam, hawthorn etc.) because the latter are apt to look 'bitty' and scattered. This is especially so when photographing in back-lighting conditions, when the sun's rays can create myriad pin-points of light through the gaps in the foliage, to say nothing of probable lens flare as a result.

Exposure assessment for back-lit leaf studies is best made by holding your meter an inch or two away, so that the light falls on it *through* the leaves. It is then up to you to decide whether you want a faithful colour record, or slightly increased or decreased colour saturation (i.e. stronger or paler colours). You may wish to emphasize the richness of colouring against a contrasting background by keeping exposure to a minimum; or conversely, to forego a little depth of colour in your subject-proper by increasing exposure in order to lighten the background and general effect.

Admirable as the miniature camera undoubtedly is, the picture-image as seen in the viewfinder is deceptively diminutive, and small unwanted details in the taking-area can consequently often go unoticed. Mis-shapen leaves can mar a close-up, and in more open scenes conflicting elements have a habit of intruding. Look beyond and around your chosen areas before you get to work with that viewfinder; projected on the screen, those little faults loom large.

Not only is the arrangement of the leaf spray within the picture area important—almost equally so are the size and disposition of the spaces between and around it. Too much space can diminish the 'pull' of the subject, too little may tend to give it a shut-in appearance. Trees such as pine, larch, ash and willow, need extra care in their pictorial treatment; so often the spaces between the leaves are far greater in area than the leaves themselves, making striking close-ups difficult to obtain.

Although sunshine makes all the difference, many successful studies have been made in dull or wet weather, while mist (but not for close-ups) lends a charm all its own. Woodlands become less dense, their lighting contrasts more manageable.

Sunsets

Wonderful sunsets often occur in September and October, presenting opportunities for brilliant transparencies. Since the spectacular effect lies almost entirely in the lighting and colouring of the sky, the exposure meter should be pointed towards this for a reading—but not directly into the rays of the sun (if this is shining at the time). The sun itself can usually be safely included in your picture if it is lightly veiled by cloud, or is not dazzling to the eye.

Having based your exposure for the sky, it follows that buildings trees, etc. and the foreground will appear as silhouettes; so it must never be forgotten that even the loveliest of sunsets can be spoilt by an ugly skyline, and this is not always easy to guard against. A flat, unbroken skyline will tend to be monotonous, and it is better to have some object such as a solitary tree, a church tower or cottage to break up this regularity with their silhouetted shapes. Whatever you select, keep it simple and unpretentious.

The effect is heightened if you can find a viewpoint which has a stretch of water in the foreground, in which a considerable expanse of sky is reflected. A carefully-thrown stone will ripple the surface of the water to prevent a mirror-like reflection that would otherwise create divided interest. Avoid half-way horizons that cut the picture into equal parts; let the sky area occupy at least two-thirds of the scene.

The after-glow that occurs when the sun sinks below the horizon is sometimes more striking that the sunset-proper; the longer exposure times involved may then necessitate the use of a tripod. Keep an eye on the dramatic lighting effects on buildings and objects *directly opposite*, these can produce rewarding shots if you work quickly. With all sunset pictures, it is worth while making extra exposures, varying these one lens stop more and one less, in order to increase the chances of getting just the right amount of luminosity and colour saturation.

• • •

FINDING WINTER PICTURES

MANY COLOUR ENTHUSIASTS still regard winter as a 'dead' season, as far as general outdoor photography is concerned—with the obvious exceptions of snow and ice subjects, and perhaps a few domestic pictures here and there. This is a pity, because there *are* many first-class pictures to be had for the taking . . . if only one has a receptive mind. Obviously, worthwhile subjects are more difficult to find. With the colder, softer light of winter, much of the impact of colour is missing; too often we see only dull greys and cheerless landscapes mainly because our 'seeing-eye' is less flexible. Remember though, that the extra concentration needed to wrest attractive shots from conditions scorned as 'unfavourable' considerably enhances your powers of observation and skill as a pictorialist.

Almost anyone can be successful with the ready-made scenes which are so abundant in other seasons; the true test of your ability comes with drab winter. Possibilities are offered by leafless trees against a sky background; indeed their beauty of form only becomes apparent in their bare state. Elm, oak, sycamore, poplar and others lend themselves to this treatment. Tall trees often look well if the camera is strongly tilted and turned deliberately to put them diagonally across the picture format, from a medium-close viewpoint.

Supplementary and/or long-focus lenses are useful for capturing the delicate detail of small things such as hazel catkins, winter berries, and the startlingly-vivid leaves which stubbornly cling to the bramble bushes in places. Light breezes may necessitate the use of shutter speeds of 1/125 sec. or faster, with the consequent opening-up of the lens bringing depth-of-field problems. It follows that while slow and medium-speed films may give stronger colouration, faster ones are usually preferable in winter.

Lighting

Winter sunshine is a fugitive thing. So often pale and wan, it helps to emphasize the coldness of a scene, and falling at a fairly low angle, its slanting rays are selective, picking out various parts of the subject to good effect. Almost invariably, shots made with even the merest hint of sunshine are preferable to those without any at all. To minimize excess blueness in dark foregrounds, a skylight or haze filter is useful. Because of the less-colourful nature of winter as a whole, open views and wide stretches are unlikely to be as satisfying to the eye as will the more-restricted scenes. A touch of contrast is sometimes desirable, to relieve the evenness of tone which generally pervades; this can take the form of a patch or colour (a person dressed in bright clothing, a painted gate or building), or simply a local dark area.

During a mild winter, in warm south-facing spots a few clumps of primroses have been known to appear as early as January or February, and certain trees bear green shoots. The pattern of the fields—some tilled, and other pastureland—can still make attractive colour shots, especially from high vantage-points in undulating country. Old barns, gates and farm implements hold promise, and a gleam of sunshine after heavy rain will give you 'different' studies of texture and patterning. Look too, for streams and ponds; reflected in them, winter sunsets can make attractive slides. It goes without saying, that the town-dweller should remember to go stoutly-shod, and keep to the country code by never leaving gates open.

Beware of the really grey day! Except as a deliberate choice for a particular subject, its overall flatness of lighting can be very deadening. Trying to liven things up by means of electronic flash may result in a measure of unnaturalness that will be generally unacceptable. Paradoxically, mist and fog (even a pea-souper) can lend themselves to picture-making with quite outstanding success. By cloaking detail and restricting visual range, these phenomena present forceful, simple—and often mysterious—shapes and planes that have pictorial values peculiarly their own. When there is a glimpse of sunshine too, almost every object has picture-potential. A practical note here: watch out for condensation on your lens!

Grasp opportunities

Wet-day pictures are by no means new to the man who uses black-and-white films, and there is scope here also for the observant colour man; a strategic sheltered viewpoint from a doorway in a busy street can give lively human-interest studies, for example. It is best to have a companion with you to hold an umbrella over your equipment if you contemplate shooting from unprotected spots. Even in a downpour, the actual raindrops are not likely to register much, but shooting against the light helps in this respeact.

Snow is so obviously a picture-maker that it needs no elaboration, but never miss the chance of photographing hoar-frost—that lovely thick rime that coats the trees, hedges and vegetation, transforming the countryside into a brittle, fascinating fairyland. Perhaps even more surprising is the way it makes practically *everything* look decorative; mundane objects in a backyard, broken fencing, wire netting—all become endowed with interesting shapes, especially if there is a little sunshine.

Such conditions occur when there are drifting banks of fog, and the temperature reaches freezing-point; the fog may lift in the morning to give a clear sky, if it doesn't, you will still find plenty to photograph. Go for the encrusted spiders' webs, the rigid hogweed, holly, and selected sprays etc. as well as general views. Fast films will give you less 'bite' than those in the slower category.

Finally, keep an eye on those winter skies. The scudding clouds, the leaden layers and violent storms, can bring variety which makes them subjects in themselves.

● ● ●

HINTS ON SLIDE SHOWS

IT PAYS TO BE painstaking in all aspects, including presentation, if you want to make the most of your slides. No matter how much you enjoy using your camera and searching out pleasing subjects, the ultimate end—where reversal colour films is concerned—lies solely in the projected picture. A first-rate slide can be spoilt by an indifferent projector, a top-class projector cannot correct the shortcomings of a badly mounted transparency, and a hastily prepared slide show will never do justice to the best of subjects.

Screens

The kind of screen upon which you project your transparencies has a great influence on their effectiveness. Just because it is possible to utilize any whitish surface or material, it is unwise to 'make do' in this manner. In the home, the hang-or-stand portable screen is quite satisfactory, provided it has side-stretchers to keep the surface taut and wrinkle-free, and there is a convenient table or support to put it on, or suitably clear wall space to hang it. For speedy erection, the sprung roller screen is

Fast and ultra-fast films allow indoor pictures to be taken without the need for flash. At night, the judicious use of one or more photoflood lamps makes things easier.

For striking close-ups of small objects such as flowers etc. a supplementary lens, extension tubes or bellows attachment (see 'Hints on close-ups' page 43) are needed. Depth-of-field is very limited, so small lens apertures are essential.

Right. Frontal flash (i.e. flash unit mounted on camera, see page 53) can be quite successful with colour films because of *colour differences* in clothing, furnishing etc.

The mellow reddish-yellow rays of late evening sunshine can produce very attractive effects; but beware of taking portraits in colour at this time of day, or your subject may look an unhealthy yellow!

Left. Subjects in back-lighting (the sun's rays coming from a point somewhere *behind* them) acquire a most attractive luminous quality, and stand out from their backgrounds. Foliage, flowers etc, become translucent.

Left. Extra care is needed with the very close approach, and the lens should be stopped down as much as possible. Subjects that have considerable depth (i.e. distance from front to rear) are usually unsuitable.

Flash (electronic or bulb) is needed for lively pictures at parties, Christmas festivities etc., plus an aptitude for choosing the right moment to shoot. Streamers, balloons and decorations give 'atmosphere' and should be included when practicable.

Examples of album pages made by mounting prints back-to-back and getting them wire- or plastic-bound (see page 144). Today, such albums are more acceptable than the conventional paste-in type. Alternatively, commercially-produced ones with slip-on pages of transparent plastic are obtainable.

hard to beat, especially when of the tripod type, which can readily be placed almost anywhere in the room.

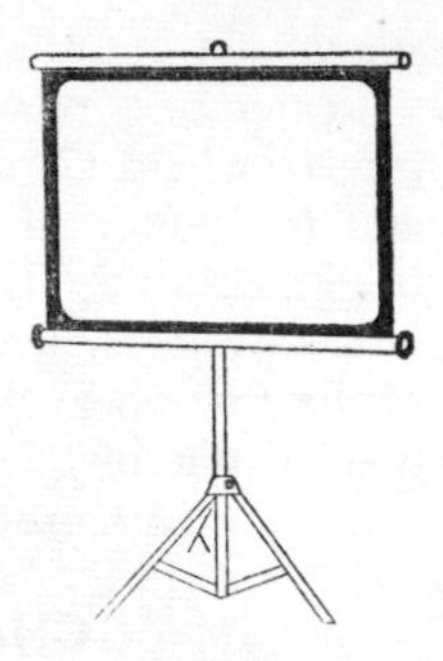

The handyman can construct a rigid one from hardboard covered with several coats of white emulsion paint, or conceal an area of plain white wall behind curtains which can be drawn aside instantly. A black border is not essential, but does provide a nice finishing touch. Naturally, to accommodate both vertical and horizontal pictures with the 35mm. format, the screen must be square in shape.

Screen surfaces

A plain matt white surface gives the best definition, and allows viewing from quite a wide angle without any serious fall-off in illumination. This surface is usually the cheapest kind. Efficiency varies with the opacity of the material used; linen, for example, is less opaque than canvas and so allows more light to *pass through*.

The newly developed plastic screens with lenticular surfaces are most effective, though in most cases a little more directional (narrow viewing angle). These give a somewhat brighter picture than ordinary matt white screens—and have, in fact, a whiter surface. Some have a blue backing to encourage brilliance, and some tend to hang unevenly unless stretched taut. Screens with beaded surfaces yield the most brilliant image *within a fairly narrow viewing angle*, and at the expense of definition (the minute beads make the picture look more grainy). Silver screens are not advisable, as they degrade the projected colours and their angle of brilliance falls off rapidly.

Sizes

In the average living-room, a 50 x 50in. screen is large enough, bearing in mind that to fill this size a projector with an 85mm. lens needs to be placed 9½ feet away, and one with 100mm. lens 11½ feet away. Picture-size also depends on the power of the lamp. It is better to have a bright picture 50in. wide than one, say, 60in. wide that is barely bright enough. Low-power projectors should not be expected to fill screens larger than 40in. square.

Remember: picture-size is governed by (1) focal length of projector lens, (2) distance from screen, (3) size of transparency, and (4) power of projector lamp (i.e. for acceptable picture brightness). Brightness is of course also governed by the aperture of the projector lens, being inversely proportional to the square of the *f* number; thus an *f*/4 lens would pass only half as much light as one of *f*/2.8. Most of todays' projectors are fitted with *f*/2.8 or *f*/3.5 lenses.

CHART OF SCREEN SIZES

From this, calculate the size of screen required in conjunction with various lenses.

Focal length of projector lens	3in. (75mm.)	3½in. (85mm.)	4in. (100mm.)	6in. (150mm.)
Screen sizes	Approximate distance from projector to screen (2 x 2in. slides)			
30 x 30in.	5ft.	5½ft.	7ft.	10½ft.
40 x 40in.	7ft.	7½ft.	9ft.	13½ft.
50 x 50in.	8½ft.	9½ft.	11½ft.	17ft.
60 x 60in.	10ft.	11½ft.	14½ft.	21ft.

For example: using a projector with 85mm. lens, a 50 x 50in. screen could be placed 9½ft. away, a 40 x 40in. screen 7½ft. away.

Projectors

With something in the region of 100 different models of 2 x 2in. slide projectors on the market—to say nothing of those of other sizes—individual choice can be difficult. For use with the popular 40in. and 50in. screens, one having a 300-watt mains voltage lamp is adequate, especially if its optical system includes an aspheric condenser. Too much screen brightness (i.e. using a very powerful projector) is undesirable—it makes colours look washed-out, and strains viewers' eyes. So a 500-watt model is best reserved for pictures wider than 50in., and for use in large rooms.

Stray light coming through the top of the lamphouse ventilating grille, and reflected from the ceiling, diminishes picture contrast and brightness; good design can keep this trouble to a minimum. Trying to mask off this stray light by means of some sort of baffle may lead to over-heating of the lamp. Evenness of screen illumination can be roughly checked with your exposure meter, without a slide in the projector gate. Judge brightness visually with an average-density slide.

Fan-cooling is unnecessary for 100- and 150-watt projectors, but essential for 300-watt models. The air stream should cool the *slides* as well as the lamp and optical system, and be directed *away* from the operator as it leaves the vents. Some projectors draw air in from the top, instead. Gate-temperatures vary considerably, with rises of 30° to 70°C above room temperature occuring in well-known makes; the higher temperatures are seldom harmful, except to damp film.

Low-voltage lamps (fed through a built-in transformer) provide more light than mains-voltage ones. So a 12 volt 100-watt lamp (for instance) gives light comparable to a 240 volt 250-watt, yet with only the heat normally generated by 100-watt. It must be stressed, however, that heat control varies greatly between different makes of projectors. Low-voltage lamps give a slightly *whiter* light, and cost less, but the transformer makes the projector higher-priced and adds to its weight.

The quartz-iodine lamp is often used nowadays (a 100-watt one can give the same output as a 300-watt mains-voltage lamp); its cool running, long life and consistent colour of light make it an attractive proposition. The small, compact filaments of low-voltage bulbs tend to give sharper pictures, because only the *centre* of the projection lens is used; in turn, this leads to less critical focusing being needed.

Automation

The fully-automatic projector has much to commend it. Slide shows go much more smoothly once the magazines are prepared, no slotted slide boxes are needed for storage—and the operator can sit at ease with the audience. Get one that permits focusing as well as slide-changing by remote control if you can afford it. On the debit side, however, such projectors are more complicated, their mechanisms add to the general noise level, sometimes trouble is experienced with card-mounted transparencies, and the essential magazines cost money.

Non-automatic projectors with their simple push-pull carriers seldom 'stick' or go wrong, but the operator has to stand and juggle with the slides, extricating them one by one from their boxes and replacing or stacking them on one side. This process carries the risk of finger-marking slides, before or after projection —a risk that is further increased as the projector body warms up, adding its heat to that already coming from the ventilating grille.

Noise

Some projectors are noisy, not only in the hum of the fan motor, but also in their slide-changing mechanism (the latter can give a most annoying 'clank-clank'). This is a disadvantage that comes with automation although a few non-auto models have noisy carriers, too. The quieter your projector is, the better your audience will enjoy the show. *Never* attempt to lessen projector noise by standing it on a soft felt pad, cushion or similar base; this will quickly cause over-heating in most cases, because it obstructs the free flow of air. A hard, smooth surface is best. To ensure that no marking occurs on polished tops of tables etc., it is a good plan to use a sheet of hardboard with felt stuck on the *underside* to prevent scratching.

Smooth slide-changing also depends upon the kind of slide mounts used. If you find that a particular sort is inclined to stick, discard it. Card mounts give trouble once they are bent; thick cover glasses somethimes jam, and loose-fitting components of plastic mounts have a habit of falling apart at the crucial moment. Other problems arise from transparencies not being flat in the film gate plane, and thus not parallel to the screen. Usually it is then only possible to keep part of the projected picture sharp. When this happens, re-mount the transparency, using either a different mount or else bind it up between cover glasses.

For protection, cover-glasses and tape binding is the best method; unfortunately, it is also the most fiddling process, requiring fastidious cleanliness and considerable patience if the results are to be spot-free. Cover-glasses—whether in preformed mounts or bound with tape—can give rise to Newton's Rings, caused through the transparency just touching the glass in places. Careful masking is usually the cure. Some glasses ('Newlo' for example) are specially etched to prevent this happening.

'Popping'

Projectors with fairly high gate temperatures cause most card-mounted transparencies to 'pop' in or out of focus—an annoying occurrence that no audience appreciates! This is because the relatively cold film base expands and buckles slightly in the warmth, the curvature pushing the film out of focus. Pre-warming the slides sometimes overcomes the trouble, and some magaine projectors do this while the slides are in the magazine chamber. With 'real cool' projectors, the problem seldom arises.

If *your* projector is prone to pop slides, you have a re-mounting job on your hands. A thin pen-knife blade pushed gently between the film (*not* the emulsion side) and the inner edge of the card window will generally allow the mount to be prised apart without damaging the transparency. Dextrous-fingered enthusiasts might prefer to slit open the card sandwich from the outer edges. Once you have opened a corner, it is easy to peel the mount apart. Never forget to wash your hands thoroughly before handling any film.

Projector maintenance

It pays to take care of your projector; a sudden jolt or knock may not affect its body, but can so easily weaken or break the lamp filament, especially if it is hot. Check to see that all is well before you start a slide show; taking things for granted may prove fatal. See that the mirror behind the lamp is correctly set and the lamp centred (if adjustable); if not, the lamp may eventually bulge through gas pressure pushing out the hot glass, or a condenser crack. Clean the condensers and heat filter from time to time, as advised in the instruction book; if overlooked, dust particles may 'bake' themselves on to the filter and become unremovable.

Surface-silvered mirrors should be touched only lightly with a very soft brush—*never* rubbed. The same advice goes for the lens. After a period of time, push-pull slide carriers may become less smooth in action; a touch of graphitc usually puts things right (rubbing the sliding parts with a soft B or BB pencil is sometimes sufficient). Mains-voltage lamps take an enormous initial surge of current when first switched on, and it will pay you to invest in a bromistor device such as the Gnome Lamp Guard to overcome this.

Always wait till the projector is cool before moving it, there is then less chance of straining or breaking the lamp filament. When using your projector in someone else's home, check the mains voltage before switching on—a simple precaution which so often gets overlooked during preparation for the show. And of course . . . keep a spare lamp handy!

Successful shows

Make sure your audience is *comfortable*. A room temperature of 65–70°F with adequate ventilation will suit most, the seating

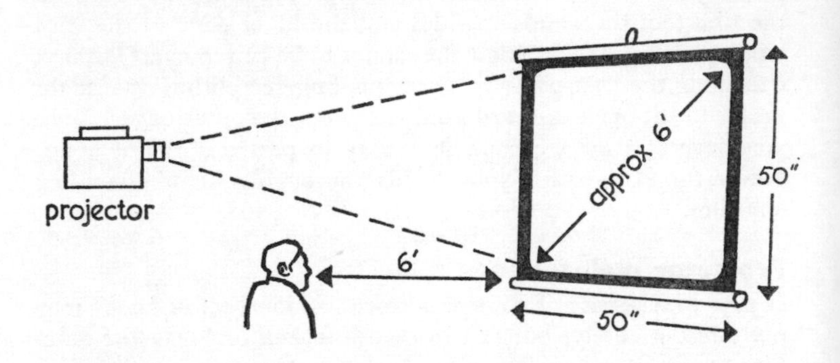

being arranged so that no one is in a draught or roasted near a fire. An open fire is a problem, and a metal fire screen may be needed to shield the projected pictures from its glow and flicker; background warmth from a convector fire is advisable.

The best viewing distance is one equal to the diagonal of the screen for pictures taken with a lens of standard focal length. Avoid seating people too much to one side. Collapsible screens should be erected well beforehand if possible, to allow them to adjust themselves to room temperature. In cold weather, warm up the projector near a fire (sudden heat in frosty conditions can sometimes crack a condenser).

Position the projector opposite the centre of the screen without a tilt if you can, just above the heads of the viewers, and see that the room is well blacked out. Keep heavy smokers away from the projector's beam; leave no trailing wires for people to fall over. Don't switch off the room lights and get started immediately, but on the other hand, don't keep your audiences waiting too long while you make last-minute adjustments or re-arrange your slides.

Quiet music from tape or record may help the preliminary settling-down process, and if you have synchro-tape facilities and carefully planned sound accompaniments *keep the volume at a reasonable level.* Taped commentaries are excellent, provided they are not rambling or pseudo-funny. Say too little rather than too much, and be prepared to answer viewers' questions. A 'family' audience will not appreciate technical jargon.

How many slides?

This is a vexed question, the answer depending largely upon the type of audience and the type of pictures; but assuming an average showing time of say, 20 seconds per slide, 100 is probably enough. Keep a few more on hand in case there is demand for them, but *never* show more than 150. While the viewers comment among themselves, all is well; if they are quiet, shorten the show.

Avoid padding-out with near-duplicates, and never show second-best slides unless you have to; edit ruthlessly. Leave the last slide projected on the screen while you turn on the room lights—don't flood the screen with the projector's naked beam. There is, perhaps, one golden rule that is applicable to all slide shows: make a good start, and make a good finish. In other words, the first slide should have impact—one that will impress immediately; and the last slide should be even more impressive. Never let a show 'fizzle out' by tailing it off with indifferent pictures.

The sequence of slides is also important; each one can be adversely affected by the slide which precedes it. Beware then, of following a shot full of strong, bright colours, with one of soft, delicate pastel colouring. The transition needs a more gradual approach. Conversely, a dramatic low-key study should not come immediately after a transparency consisting mainly of lighter tones. Comparisons, too, are inevitable if and when you mix shots from different makes of film; such mixing must be done with great care.

TIPS THAT HELP

Remember that three views of one scene are NOT better than one.
Keep 'family' shots strictly for family audiences.
Arrange everything before seating the viewers if you can.
Make sure all your slides are in correct sequence—and right way up!
Position the projector square-on to the screen, and not at an angle.
Keep a spare projection lamp handy.
Check the mains voltage when giving a show in someone else's home.
Show only your best slides.

• • •

TIPS FOR CAMERA CARE

An ever-ready case is virtually an essential item for camera protection against the elements and general handling. Although a neck-sling is often more convenient during shooting sessions, don't neglect that all-important case; keep it in good condition with suitable polish or leather dressing.

Co-axial flash sockets and their connecting plugs are delicately made. Connections made in a hurry, or without due care, may result in damage or misalignment; disconnecting by pulling quickly on the cable is liable to have the same effect in time. The more recent cable-less flash units with their shoe-centre contacts eliminate this possibility.

Interchangeable lenses should *never* be stood on their 'business ends' when changing over, as this is likely to damage the focusing flange by denting or eventual wear. Lay them down gently, making sure they cannot roll, preferably not on a hard surface—nor a dusty one.

Always keep the instruction book that was supplied with your camera—and put it where you can find it at a moment's notice. It's surprising how frequently little points crop up in connection with camera operation, and that booklet becomes a handy reference. In addition, should you ever wish to sell your equipment at a later date, the original instructions are always appreciated.

The rapid wind lever on most of today's miniatures is a substantial affair. It is unwise, however, to put any unnecessary strain on this should the film be winding tightly, or the end reached. At the best, torn perforations are likely to result; at the worst, the inner mechanism may be damaged.

A lens cap is not a gimmick, but a commonsense protection for the 'eye' of your camera. Except when actually in use, no lens should be left uncovered. If you haven't got a lens cap (or have lost it) buy one that fits properly. A loose one will keep falling off, and one that is too tight will be a nuisance.

Camera manufacturers usually advise against leaving the shutter set for long periods, particularly in the case of the faster speeds (where the spring tension is greater). Whenever possible therefore, make it a habit to see that your shutter is not wound if you do not anticipate using the camera for a week or two. A few days' interval is seldom harmful if you leave it set on one of the slower speeds—1/30sec. for example.

A blower-brush is a worth-while investment. It efficiently removes those stray fibres and dust particles which invariably find their way inside cameras. The brush should be kept clean by storing it in a polythene bag.

It is better to check your camera's rangefinder from time to time, than to rely implicity on its accuracy year after year. Robust as most instruments are, the delicate setting can occasionally 'wander', and while slight inaccuracies may not matter when photographing distant objects, with close viewpoints and large lens apertures focusing errors are often fatal.

Sunshine can be the making of a picture, but it is inadvisable to leave any camera exposed to its strong rays for any length of time. Direct sunshine has in fact been known to burn pin-holes in fabric shutter blinds, the uncovered lens (focused at infinity) acting as a 'burning glass'.

Take care when screwing your camera onto a tripod; a crossed or damaged thread might easily mean costly replacements on either, or both. This is especially applicable when using a tripod with a fixed top, the non-rotating screw then necessitates *extra* care. Watch out too, for tripods which might force their tops into the camera base because their threads project deeper than those of the camera bush.

Some older cameras have a 'weak spot' in their design or construction. For example: 'The delayed action device should not be used with the shutter set at 1/500 *or* 1/1,000 *sec.'; or 'The shutter speed setting dial should not be rotated past a certain limit'. Respect such limitations and keep them fixed in your mind; never 'experiment' to see what might happen by ignoring them.*

Should you ever have the misfortune to get your camera wet in the rain, dry it immediately with a fluffless cloth, and leave it near a source of steady *low* warmth overnight. Never put it away in its ever-ready case if there is even a suspicion of damp remaining.

Remember that the film pressure plate and the film channel are in direct contact with every film you use. The slightest damage to either, or any roughening of their surfaces by grit particles, is likely to produce 'tram lines' (scratches traversing the length of the film).

While it is sometimes possible to get rid of scratches on the film back by polishing, nothing can be done about scratched emulsion.

If your camera has the tripod bush near or at one end of the base, it is best to construct some form of cradle to support it and so minimize overhang and strain. Commercial cradles are sometimes obtainable for certain makes, and are a good buy.

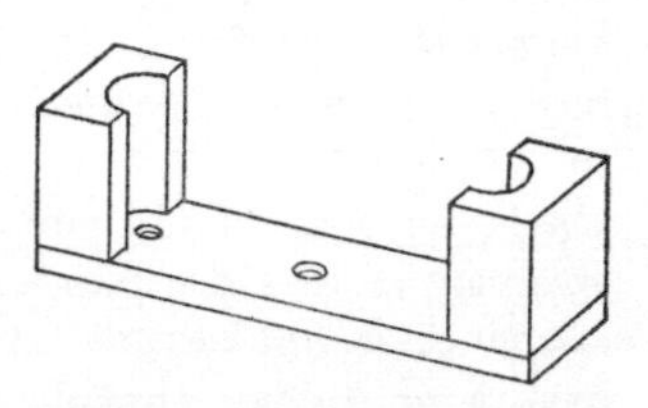

Built-in photo-electric exposure meters are made to withstand a fair amount of jolting, but the wise photographer sees to it that no such treatment occurs; nor is the meter exposed to strong light for long periods, which might then weaken the response of the selenium cell.

The term 'hard coating' is relative; optical glass is soft, and that bloom or coating will not stand for heavy-handed cleaning. Never touch the surface with your fingers, and use either lens tissue or a very soft brush for cleaning—only when necessary. Once scratched badly, a lens has to be repolished—a process that usually alters the curvature slightly.

Beware of leaving your camera unattended on a tripod—even outdoors with no one in sight; a sudden gust of wind is all that is needed to topple it. When photographing groups, or whenever there are people nearby, make sure there is someone to keep a guarding hand on the tripod while you take exposure readings etc. The higher the tripod, the greater the risk of it being knocked over.

When loading up cassettes from bulk lengths of film, there is often a great temptation to wind on as much film as possible, in order to get perhaps 40 or more exposures. This practice may result in emulsion abrasions due to the extra-tight winding within the cassette, and can impose strain on the camera rewind crank and/or rapid wind lever. It's plainly false economy.

Sometimes the accessory shoe on some cameras tends to be on the tight side, with consequential risk of scratching accessories or the camera top when removing finders, flash units etc. from the shoe. To ease matters, rub inside the shoe and on the feet of the accessories with a soft pencil, avoiding the centre flash (cable-less) contact if one is fitted. Alternatively, the lightest smear of silicone furniture polish may be used.

On no account should you ever attempt to dismantle a lens, or any part of it. Once tampered with, even superficially, its performance is unlikely to be improved. Rotating front elements have a multi-start thread, collapsible lenses having a packing; both should give many years of trouble-free service.

Use a polish-impregnated cloth to keep the chrome and metal finishes of your camera clean and sparkling. Liquid polishes or pastes may leave slight deposits which would have to be brushed out afterwards; too much hard rubbing may 'brass' the finish.

When you are not using your camera, store it carefully. Put it in a dry place, such as a cupboard or drawer, still in its ever-ready case or gadget bag (avoid airing cupboards). For further protection, a small bag of silica gel or a piece of the special rust-preventing paper now available may be included. Some enthusiasts like to enclose everything in polythene bags.

Be wise—insure your equipment against possible damage, loss, and theft. Premiums are reasonable, and claims are dealt with promptly.

Small scratches and abrasions on the leatherette portion of your camera may be touched out by careful application of suitable leather dye.

If your camera has a built-in CdS exposure meter, remember to inspect from time to time the mercury cell which powers it. Because this cell has a long working life, it is all too easy to forget this simple check to guard against possible chemical deterioration that might damage the camera. Remember too, not to touch the cell's contacts, otherwise a slight film may be deposited on them.

TAKING BLACK-AND-WHITE PICTURES

THE MODERN COLOUR FILM literally 'sees' the scene before it in much the same way as the human eye, and many people can be more easily satisfied in this medium; but with black-and-white film it is quite another matter. Remember your early attempts at photographing the 'pretty' scenes—the colourful gardens, those lovely open views? How different they looked when translated into a compressed collection of greys and blacks on a small area of white paper!

That is the snag with monochrome film; one just *has* to learn to visualize everything *minus* its colour-content. Once this is done, you're half-way on the road to success. It is not an accomplishment that can be acquired overnight, nor is it simple. Some lucky ones have an instinctive flair for it; some find that it always eludes them. Usually it takes quite a bit of time—and experience.

Have you watched an artist at work sketching a landscape? He has a dodge well worth copying—from time to time he studies the scene before him *through half-closed eyes*. This has the effect of subduing a good deal of the fussy detail, enabling him to appraise the merits or shortcomings of the shapes and masses.

All of which could obviously be helpful to photographers—and is often far easier and quicker than assessing the pictorial possibilities by squinting through the camera viewfinder, especially one of the smaller optical ones. But the trick does even more: it tends to diminish the brightness of the various colours. Saturated yellows, light blues and the lighter hues generally, are less affected than the deeper colours. Much depends upon the prevailing light, the colour grouping and its juxtaposition.

Viewing filters

As a practical aid in suppressing colour, a viewing filter can be used; this is simply to look through *not* to place on the camera lens. Ilford recommend three types of these: (1) Neutral density filters—for lowering the general brightness of a scene, (2) Monochromatic viewing filter (MV)—a dark yellow filter that 'kills' all colour differences in a scene, leaving only differences in brightness (sometimes used by film technicians when arranging lighting on studio sets), and (3) Photographic vision (panchromatic) filter. This last-named filter is purple in colour, and converts the eye's sensitivity to that of a panchromatic emulsion; by viewing through it *and* the filter to be used on the lens, the final effect may be judged.

Similarly, among Kodak's 'Wratten' range of filters they list a Wratten No. 90. Olive in colour, this monochromatic viewing filter reduces colour brightness to assist the study of tone values. Whichever course you adopt, a certain amount of experience is necessary before the full benefits can be appreciated.

Broadly speaking, it is the impact of the *vivid* colours that can so often mislead the pictorialist into thinking that certain scenes and subjects will make attractive monochrome shots. Pale pastel shades have far less 'pull' or influence, yet oddly enough, these same shades usually contribute greatly to the overall appeal of almost any subject, whether it is photographed in black-and-white or in colour.

Many expert photographers advise against taking colour and monochrome shots at the same sessions, as the eye needs to 'see' differently for each. Working in both mediums side-by-side as it were, can adversely affect pictorial perception for either—or both. It pays, therefore, to stick to one at a time if you can. Human nature being what it is however, this dictum is seldom upheld in practice when attractive subjects and good lighting are encountered!

The *intensity* of colours, and their subsequent values when translated into monochrome, are also dependent upon lighting. Sunshine, so desirable in most cases, by 'brightening-up' the colours sometimes makes it more difficult to visualize the black-and-white possibilities of a subject. This is particularly noticeable in the case of garden studies, flower beds etc.; here it should be remembered that white and light-coloured blooms are more suitable.

Colour filters

Quite a number of people seem to regard colour filters as being merely a means of capturing clouds; in other words, simply to give tone to a blue sky. A filter will of course lighten the tone values of any object of its own colouring, and darken those of complementary colouring. It is as well to bear in mind therefore,

FILTERS FOR BLACK-AND-WHITE PHOTOGRAPHY

Filter	*Factor*	*Lightens*	*Darkens*	*Use*
Light Yellow	x $1\frac{1}{2}$	Yellow and Green slightly	Blue slightly	Sports subjects. Short exposures. Improved colour.
Medium Yellow	x 2	Yellow and Green	Blue/Violet	Sky correction. Clouds. Distance. Landscapes. Seascapes. etc.
Deep Yellow	x 3	Yellow. Green slightly	Blue/Violet	Sky correction (stronger). Clouds. Distance. Landscapes. Seascapes. etc.
Yellow-Green	x 2	Yellow and Green	Blue/Violet	Good general purpose filter. Suitable for outdoor portraits, landscapes.
Light Green	x 2	Green	Red, Orange. Blue slightly	Landscapes. Foliage. General.
Medium Green	x 3	Green	Red, Orange. Blue slightly	Similar to Light Green but with stronger correction.
Orange	x 4 to 5	Red, Orange and Yellow	Blue/Violet Blue/Green	Haze penetration (clarifies distant views). Strong sky effects.
Red	x 8	Red, Orange and Yellow	Blue/Violet Blue/Green	Pseudo night-effects, extra-strong contrasts in sky.
Blue	x $1\frac{1}{2}$	Blue, Blue/Green and Blue/Violet	Orange and Red	Corrects colour balance in artificial light portraiture.
U.V. (Ultra Violet)	x 0	Eliminates Ultra-Violet		Snowscapes and high altitudes.

Note: the above is not a complete list, but covers those in general use.

that strong filters such as orange and red can affect the monochrome film to the extent of producing black, empty shadows, when the prevailing lighting is in itself contrasty. Learning to 'see' like the film emulsion thus also entails judging the resultant effect of certain filters when used for specific subjects.

To give another example: using a 3x green filter for a sunny lanscape can often produce over-light tones for grassy stretches and hedges. Although it also lightens tree foliage, this usually has the contrasting tone of the sky to prevent it merging into the general scene too much. Many find the tonal rendering produced by a 2x or 3x yellow filter more acceptable in such cases.

There are a number of other factors that can mar the intended picture. Disregarding exposure errors, incorrect focusing, subject-blurr and camera shake, we are left with (1) bad lighting, (2) poor viewpoint and (3) uninteresting subject, singly or collectively, as possible sources of disappointnemt. Each of these is associated with the other two—an indifferent subject can be saved by dramatic lighting or imaginative viewpoint, an unusual subject succeed even in flat lighting, and so on. One last hazard remains: film processing and printing must be right . . . . quite a list for the perfectionist to master!

• • •

HINTS ON FOCUSING

IN THEORY, FOCUSING a camera lens should be a straightforward, mechanical business requiring no detailed explanation. In practice—at least, where pictorialism is concerned—certain aspects must be considered, especially in the case of the 35mm. miniature camera with its great depth-of-field. Stop for stop, it gives a deeper zone of sharp focus than that provided by larger instruments. In fact it has been said (and not without some justification) that pictures taken with miniatures can be recognized as such because of their tendency to all-over sharpness.

Even when used at full aperture, the lenses fitted to today's modest-priced cameras perform commendably well in most instances, yet the advantages of differential (or 'selective') focusing are not always exploited as much as they could be. It stands to reason that distant objects in a general scene will not appear to be far away if they are recorded as bitingly-sharp as the foreground, despite their smaller scale. Differential focusing ensures that the subject-proper is sharply rendered, while other elements in the picture are less sharp; thus the subject is literally made to 'stand out' from the rest, given emphasis as the main interest, and accompanying details are slightly subdued.

But it is not an infallible recipe for success in pictorialism, nor is it suitable for all kinds of subjects. This is particularly so with colour photography; on the screen, strong, saturated colours fuzzily recorded can be very irritating and distracting, especially if their areas are at all large. It therefore becomes largely a question of *when* selective focusing will help, and with which subjects. Incidentally, the technique becomes virtually automatic in poor lighting conditions, when full-aperture working (and resultant decrease in depth-of-field) is often inevitable.

Zone of sharpness

It must be remembered too that at distances greater than, say 25ft., the 'standard' 45 or 50mm. lens on most miniatures gives quite a deep zone of sharpness when used fully open, so the effect of selective focusing is really only evident with close and medium-close subjects. This narrows down the field of application somewhat, and it is obvious that you cannot use it with large subjects such as buildings etc. because you are forced to choose a more distant viewpoint in order to cover them adequately. For instance: at 50ft., a 45mm. lens at *f*/2.8 has a sharpness zone extending from 29 to 175ft., while a 50mm. lens focused to the same distance gives sharpness from 32 to 120ft. at *f*/2.8. Things are very different at 8ft. away—still at this aperture, the lenses now have sharpness zones from 7ft. 2in. to 9ft., and 7ft. 4in. to 8ft. 9½in. respectively, i.e. less than 2ft.

It follows that if and when you can photograph a subject with the main motif of interest at 8ft. or closer, the effect of differential focusing can be striking; but there is not of course, a *sudden* change from sharp to unsharpness at any time—it is a gradual, harmonious conversion. There is however, one 'must' You *must* focus accurately in all cases, or you will accent the wrong part of the picture, and to have the background sharper than your subject can be disastrous. This is no problem for those whose cameras have rangefinders or reflex focusing, but if yours hasn't, and you are working merely a few feet away, there is no margin for errors. It will pay you to measure the distance whenever convenient, rather than rely solely upon your own judgment. At *f*/2 the need for accurate focusing is even more vital, depth-of-field being just a matter of inches at the closer distances.

The technique of using larger apertures has another benefit to offer: it allows faster shutter speeds to be employed, and so reduces the risk of camera shake. People who have got into the habit of firing at speeds of 1/25, 1/30, 1/50 or 1/60th. of a second for hand-held shots are apt to get a shock when they suddenly discover the improvement in sharpness of pictures made at faster shutter speeds!

The right time

The question of *when* to use differential focusing is a complex one, no hard-and-fast rules can be applied; lighting, type of subject, background, setting, treatment—all play their part in influencing the decision. Whenever you are faced with a 'fussy' background full of unwanted detail and objects which in no way contribute to the intended picture, or whenever the general setting around a comparatively small object is unsuitable, open up your lens aperture and thus keep the subject in an island of sharpness.

Be careful though, with unsharp foregrounds; if too blurred or forceful, or large in area, they can be irritating. When this is unavoidable, it is usually better to keep them to a minimum when making the print, or masking-off the transparency in the case of colour film. Regarding lighting: with 'deep' backgrounds full of varying planes, side-lighting can prove awkward, since it throws these planes into marked relief and accentuates them. In such instances, flat or frontal lighting may be preferable. Back-lighting is often ideal, as it naturally isolates the subject and puts the background in shadow; allied to careful differential focusing, this condition can produce pseudo-stereoscopic relief.

With outdoor portraiture, backgrounds should normally be subordinate to the person photographed, yet many miniaturists work at apertures around *f*/4 to *f*/8 when full or nearly-full apertures would improve matters in this respect. When suitable backgrounds are hard to find, just keep your subject *well away* from the wall, fence or what-have-you, and move in close with your camera lens at full aperture; results will then at least be presentable. (see Illustrations on page 145).

Sense of distance

General scenes come into a different category. You have to decide whether you want to convey a sense of distance, or whether you want the whole thing sharp. A woodland study, for instance, would lack atmosphere and depth if the farthest tree looked as sharp as those in front, but an open panorama would be only partly successful if the distant detail appeared blurred. Similarly, a 'record' shot of any particular spot normally requires all-over sharpness; the same applies to interiors—they should be full of biting detail in most cases.

This does not necessarily mean that you have to go to the other extreme and stop down to *f*/16 or *f*/22; these apertures (where miniature cameras are concerned, at any rate) can be reserved for close-ups, copying etc. Work in conjunction with the depth-of-field scale engraved on your camera; this most useful feature is often overlooked. Reference to it will quickly show the most suitable aperture to choose in questionable circumstances to cover the whole subject adequately.

You want a foreground cottage or tree to be recorded as sharply as the scene a little further away? Don't automatically stop down a lot and work at a shutter speed of, say, 1/30th second. Consult that depth-of-field scale; it's the work of a moment to arrange things so that you select the largest aperture which will do the trick at a given distance, and allow perhaps 1/100th. second to be used instead. Focus first on the foreground object and note its distance, do the same for the middle-distance, then see that depth-of-field covers both when you decide on the aperture. Your exposure meter will indicate the shutter speed to use with that aperture. Once again, if you have no rangefinder or focusing aid, it may take longer, and you will probably have to estimate the distances.

For those whose cameras take interchangeable lenses, the depth-of-field scale can be invaluable, as differential focusing is far more pronounced with long-focus lenses.

• • •

TIPS ON COMPOSITION

Whatever the subject of your picture, try to arrange to have only one main point of interest, and let everything else included become subordinated to it. This is usually achieved by careful *selection*—selection of viewpoint, taking-distance, subject-arrangement in viewfinder, amount included, lighting, and sometimes differential focusing.

Watch the horizon. Make sure that it does not divide your picture into two equal parts, nor sweep from one side to the other without any verticals to break its continuity. This is difficult to overcome with panoramic views and seascapes etc. unless some foreground object sufficiently tall can be found. Sloping horizons in seascapes are unforgivable.

To achieve unity, the main mass in a pictorial composition should normally have some secondary, smaller mass or shadow tone to balance it—not in an obvious, geometric way, but so that the whole looks 'correct' and satisfying to the eye. Exceptions may occur, as for instance when deliberate 'central placing' is resorted to for effect, or when the distribution of the various masses is subtly repetitive.

Reflections in water can be most attractive, but if they are almost exact duplicates of the subject-proper, divided-interest results. The

trick is to break up the duplication by throwing in a stone to ripple the image. Sometimes reflections are more interesting than the subject itself, then they should be given precedence in the picture area.

A dark foreground is a useful compositional device to employ in picture-making, and one which lends itself to many landscape subjects. It not only acts as a stable base for the whole composition, but also helps to stop the eye from wandering out of the print.

The limits or outer edge of a picture are also part of its composition. Those open spaces and 'holes' inside the margin need to have variety in shape and area. Don't let the outer limits cut off an important part of the picture in the drive for simplicity—a foreground tree needs its base; a person's legs should not end at the ankles.

As a rule, diverse objects, or those of greatly differing type, make pictorial arrangement difficult; deliberate inclusion of such objects can give rise to incongruity, and destroy unity.

Horizontal lines make for peacefulness and placidity; diagonals suggest liveliness and activity, while vertical lines indicate strength and stability. A curved line is always more interesting than a straight one. Leading lines should never encourage the eye out *of a picture, nor traverse straight across from one side to another.*

Wherever two or more leading lines meet or intersect, that is a 'strong' point of the picture. Make sure that these strong points fall in satisfying positions, never too near the picture edge, and that there are not too many of them in one composition. Scattered strong points eliminate unity by attracting the eye from one spot to another.

Low viewpoints emphasize outlines, and tend to increase the subject's importance by lifting it out of its surroundings. Changing your viewpoint, a little to the left or right, nearer or farther back, can change the whole aspect and balance.

Sloping lines appearing near the edges of a picture exert a strong pull to that side, and can be distracting to the eye. When deciding the picture's limits, care should be taken to keep such elements nearer to the centre when possible, or excluded altogether if they are unimportant to the subject.

Provided that there are no 'give-away' verticals such as buildings, or a natural horizontal such as water, sometimes a scene can gain added interest by a sideways *tilt; either by tilting the camera at the time of taking, or by slewing the paper when printing. Landscapes, figure studies and portraiture may be suitable for this treatment.*

With architecture, tops of doorways, windows, arches etc. should not touch the edge of the picture—a certain amount of masonry should be shown above them, or else the tops excluded. Similarly, the bases of archways, pillars and doorways should not coincide with the base of the picture, nor preferably be shown too close to it.

Avoid having lines running exactly into the corners of your print, since these are certain to lead the eye out of the picture. If the lines are straight, and the tones in the angles be contrasty, their combined attraction value is the strongest possible—to the detriment of the subject-proper.

• • •

HINTS ON WINNING COMPETITIONS

FROM TIME TO TIME, photographic competitions are announced in the national and photographic press, offering substantial prizes and attracting many thousands of entrants. Not only do these contests foster the competitive spirit, they also help and encourage people to improve their pictorial standards and photographic technique. Once a prize has been won, one feels that a definite step forward has been made, and this advancement spurs the winner on to even greater achievements.

It is wrong to think that you must have expensive equipment in order to stand a chance; indeed, most of the 'popular' competitions are organized mainly for those who have modest-priced cameras, so that practically every member of the family can compete. Limitations in equipment may be felt only in the 'specialized' contests sponsored by camera manufacturers, film manufacturers, photographic journals etc. where winning entries have to be technically good as well as striking in subject.

Picture-making is a personal thing; what one person considers good, another might dislike. Judges are human, and some look for one thing in a photograph, some for another. Furthermore, it is as well to remember that there is *always* an element of luck about it. Freshness of approach is a great asset, and in this respect, the man who only takes photographs now and again has the advantage over someone who is constantly using his camera, and who thereby tends to keep to one style, one form of treatment.

Half the battle lies in knowing your camera so well that its use is more or less automatic, and of course, if yours *is* an automatic camera, matters are made easier still! When you are completely familiar with your instrument and all its controls, and can handle it without fiddling and checking in an undecided manner, you are free to give your subject(s) your undivided attention and concentration. With moving subjects, even slow ones, hesitation in operating the camera can often lose that 'right moment'.

At the risk of repetition, it must be stressed that probably more pictures are ruined through camera-shake than any other cause. Maybe you are one of the few who can work with shutter speeds as slow as 1/30 or 1/25 sec. and consistently get sharp negatives; it is better to play safe however, and keep to 1/60 or 1/100 sec. as your slowest hand-held exposures whenever you can. Given two pictures of a similar subject, one needle-sharp and the other slightly blurred all over due to camera-shake, it's obvious which one any competition judge would choose. (This should not be confused with differential focusing, whereby a selected part of the pictures would be sharply focused while the rest remained out-of-focus).

Watch the rules

It is surprising how many entries get rejected simply because they do not conform to the rules. No matter how good your picture may be, it won't stand a chance unless it complies with the rules in every way, especially perhaps, in the case of colour. Sometimes *unmounted* transparencies are asked for, alternatively, cardboard mounts might be accepted; usually, transparencies need to be correctly 'spotted' for projection . . . and always labelled with your name and address besides the title.

There is one (unwritten) rule which should *never* be forgotten: beware of imitating photographs which have won prizes previously, particularly if in that same competition. If it is an annual contest, it's no use hoping that slight variations of last year's winning subjects, or the year before, are likely to ring the bell again with the judges. Keep off them entirely. For instance: suppose a picture of a little girl holding a kitten was a prizewinner, don't submit similar shots with little boys and puppies. This does not mean that these *subjects* will not win again; it's the way you introduce them into the picture that counts. Similar attitudes with similar material is the theme you have to avoid.

Try not to include hackneyed scenes—those famous beauty spots which have been so much photographed that everyone is all too familiar with them. No one questions the attractions and loveliness of such subjects, it's just that it's rather like flogging a dead horse.

If the rules stipulate that entries should be sent in an unsealed envelope, don't conveniently overlook this and seal yours up. The people who have to handle those envelopes will probably put yours on one side to deal with later; it *could* happen that your entry, through being separated from the others, gets overlooked or mixed with used wrappings and thrown away. A crumpled, bent picture will not do justice to your work; always send your photographs sandwiched between two pieces of stout cardboard, preferably an inch or two larger all round for protection in the post. Flexible, corrugated card packing is no use, the cardboard must be rigid.

Should you have to stick an entry coupon on the back of each print (or a caption), don't use gum or paste, these will cause the print to cockle. Rubber mountant such as 'Cow' or transparent Sellotape are better. Lay the print face down on a hard smooth surface when you print your name and address on it, otherwise it may indent through to the front; this is particularly liable to happen with thin singleweight glossy prints.

Print sizes

Competition rules generally state the size limits of entries, or at least indicate the recommended sizes. These may be from whole-plate to 15 x 12in.—larger than this is seldom allowed among the popular press contests. It does not necessarily follow that the biggest pictures stand the best chance of winning. Suppose you decide to submit a head-and-shoulders study of a baby or child; enlarged to 15 x 12in. the over-all charm of expression and attitude is easily missed unless it is viewed from a fair distance. During the initial sorting-out process, entries are usually handled at a desk or table, and there just isn't time for every large print to be individually propped up and viewed from across the room.

It may seem that this handicaps *all* the large prints; in a sense perhaps it does, but not so much as those where the subject begins to approach life-size, as in the case of the head-and-shoulders' study. General scenes, open and semi-open views suffer less because they are reproduced smaller in relative subject-scale. If your particular print shows *all* the child, or even three-quarter length, the close viewing distance will be of less consequence. Later, when numbers are whittled down and final judging takes place, those big prints will come into their own by being viewed from the correct distance.

Whatever your subject however, you will seldom be wrong if you submit whole-plate or 10 x 8in. prints. Viewed on a table at distances of one to two feet, these sizes are very acceptable—they look 'right' and are of pleasing proportions. Square pictures can be conveniently printed on these same papers, leaving a margin at the base if you wish; alternatively, 10 x 10in. square borderless prints made by trimming 12 x 10in. paper can be most effective.

Captions

Competition organizers sometimes want to know how and why you took a photograph. If they do, be brief and factual; no one wants to wade through a long and rambling description or read a covering letter. A really apt caption can put the finishing touch to a photograph that portrays humour, action or emotion etc. A long, hackneyed or 'forced' caption can spoil everything. Fortunately, captions are not often required, and if none is asked for, don't imagine you will be 'putting one over the other chap' by adding a few well-chosen words—it's the photograph that counts, every time. Simply print legibly in block letters any relevant details such as place-names, make of camera, film etc. or other stipulated data in the rules, not forgetting of course, your name and address.

Bear in mind that it is frequently a consideration that copyright of the winning photographs becomes the property of the competition sponsors, so you must be prepared to part with the negative (or transparency); or you may be allowed to keep it for your own personal use—it must not be reproduced or loaned without first obtaining permission from the copyright owners.

When to send?

When competitions run for lengthy periods, the big prizes being awarded at the finish, and intermediate ones throughout, there is some conjecture as to which is the *best time* to send in prints—the start, the finish, or some time in-between. A lot depends upon the kind of contest, and the time of the year. If it is a popular one with several classes of subjects, there is nearly always a flood of entries after the first two weeks or so. Numbers might decline after half-way through the allotted period, with an even bigger rush of entries as it draws to a close. Between half-way and three-quarters therefore seems to be a good time.

Things are usually different with 'holiday' contests. Photographs taken in earlier years are frequently barred, and entries flow in fairly steadily from the start, increasing in volume until the close of the contest. In such cases, early holidaymakers with cameras might gain one of the initial prizes against less fierce competition than later on, otherwise it is probably immaterial *when* entries are sent in. Smaller competitions, and those organized by photographic journals, are less affected by surges of entries; it is then a matter of sending your pictures when it best suits you.

In *all* competitions, this sound advice applies: don't leave it to the last possible minute unless you are forced to. Rushing round preparing work against the clock is a bad policy; it is so easy to overlook something, and so hard to give of your best.

How many prints?

Some people try to increase their chances of success by submitting an avalanche of prints when there are no restrictions on the number of photographs you can send in. This is wrong. It is made easier by the modern miniature which takes 36 pictures (or 72 in the case of half-frame cameras) in one loading; this economy in film due to the small size, encourages the owner to take several shots of each subject where only one would probably be taken with a larger instrument.

For sequence shots of people, animals, action etc. this practice has much to commend it; it is not advisable though, to send in several slightly differing pictures of the same subject. Choose the best one of the batch, or, if you can't make up your mind about it, then at least restrict it to two, preferably taken from widely diverse viewpoints. Never lose sight of the fact that it is *quality*, not quantity, that counts.

In any case, it is better to submit, say, four lots of three rather than twelve in one go, or even two lots of six. If you have an outstanding photograph (and these are the ones that usually win), send it in by itself. In this way it will not weaken the chances of the rest of your work, as it would if they were judged side by side. When the rules restrict you to three only, it is sometimes assumed that you will send this number in one entry. Should this be optional, then make three entries, sending only one at a time. Given any luck, this gives your work three separate appearances at intervals, instead of appearing in front of the judges once only. This is particularly the case when you submit in only one section of a contest, and your subject(s) similar.

Specialized competitions

The competitions which are arranged by photographic journals, societies and clubs, demand photographs of a high technical standard and finish, and snapshotters and newcomers would be out of their depth unless a beginners' section was included. Print quality, composition, treatment and presentation are every bit as important as the subject-matter in these specialized contests, and judging is usually more ruthless. Since the main object of photographic publications is to raise the technical and pictorial standards of their readers, most of whom are very competent photographers anyway, it stands to reason that competition is very fierce. When the print itself is beyond reproach, then subject and treatment must have that little extra something which the others haven't got. This *may* be a question of luck, but more often it is due to careful thought and observation before pressing the button.

Unless the rules specify glossy prints, it is wiser to use paper surfaces that suit the subject. For instance, portraits can look very cold and impersonal on glossy paper; a 'Royal', stipple or lustre surface often being much more suitable. Cream-based papers, especially those of the chlorobromide variety, add warmth. As a general guide: for subjects dependent upon lots of sharp, biting detail, use glossy or royal surfaces. For broad effects, use the more open-textured papers such as rough lustre.

Subjects

In many photographic contests the subject-scope is fairly wide; sometimes there are no set subjects, prizes being awarded simply for the best pictures. This can be tricky, because faced with a scene, a child picture and an animal study each of equal excellence in its respective sphere, who can say which is the winner? Under these circumstances, only a positively outstanding photograph can make things easier for the judges, otherwise their personal preferences are bound to complicate matters.

Again, whenever 'beautiful views' are listed, people are apt to think it is only necessary to turn their cameras towards some renowned panoramic vista, press the button, and the chances of winning a prize are good. How wrong this attitude is! If the view in question is a well-known beauty-spot, it is surely obvious that *they* will not be the only ones to photograph it. The sad truth is that landscapes (or 'views') are most difficult subjects

GUIDE TO SUBJECT-POPULARITY IN GENERAL COMPETITIONS

Rating	*Subject*
*****	Children with animals—appealing subject material. Children at play etc.—no posed set-ups, capture natural attitudes. Babies—avoid static, 'ordinary' pictures. Pretty girls, bathing beauties etc.—attractive poses necessary.
****	Human interest studies—people gossiping, working etc.—*not* camera-conscious. Young animals—kittens, puppies etc. Pictorial studies, scenes etc.—must be first-class technique. Humorous pictures—a difficult subject to portray. Holiday scenes, incidents etc.
***	Action studies—sport etc., must be striking. Character portraits. Unusual pictures. Night studies—must be pictorially striking. Domestic and/or zoo animals—must be interesting in pose, lighting etc.
**	Still life studies—must be unusual. Table-top studies—must be original. Buildings etc.—must have pictorial aspect.
*	'Record' shots etc. with little or no pictorial value. Ancient monuments, statues.

in which to succeed; it is all too easy to crowd in too much.

While no rule-of-thumb can bc given, in the majority of cases *simplicity* generally scores. The key words 'boldness and simplicity' should be applied to all competition subjects whenever possible. In addition, your pictures should tell a story, preferably with a 'twist'. This means that you should try to capture some fresh angle, some slightly different approach. In the case of human-interest subjects a ready trigger-finger and a pre-set camera will do much to increase the chance of getting a 'lucky shot' that packs a punch. With children, it pays to think of ideas in advance if you can, and make amusing incidents happen; but in building-up ideas it is essential to let all actions and expressions be natural ones, and in no way posed. There is always an element of luck involved.

Beware of the bogey of fashion! Before you send in prints from negatives made in previous years, make sure there are no tell-tale features which 'date' them. Girls' dress and hair styles change quickly and can spoil things; street-scenes with cars, posters etc, may have a useful life of only a year or two before their age becomes evident. Beware too, when the subject-list includes 'humorous pictures'—a funny photograph is a difficult proposition, a really funny one is extremely rare. This is probably because humour depends on movement to put it over, and at best a still photograph can only suggest this. Dressing up people or animals in odd attire does not provoke mirth: incongruity might.

• • •

HINTS ON PHOTOGRAPHING ANIMALS

ANIMALS STUDIES RANK HIGH as a popular subject with many camera owners. It is simple enough to get 'record' shots of the family pet sitting around: for really striking, rewarding pictures however, certain precautions have to be observed. Failures are usually the fault of the human element—animals are never camera-conscious, and seldom awkward or clumsy—and all true animal lovers will know that success lies largely in the ability to *understand* animals. In addition, the cameraman must be extremely patient, nimble and alert to catch 'the right moment'.

As animals' movements are more or less unpredictable, they are virtually 'action' subjects unless you take them in sleepy, relaxed moods. It is therefore best to get them outdoors in good light, and be prepared to shoot off several frames; medium-speed film is often fast enough for all but the liveliest creatures. Fast film, of course, has its advantages, allowing smaller lens apertures (with their greater depth-of-field) and faster shutter speeds to be used.

Kittens

The lovable antics and air of helpless surprise make the kitten a 'natural' subject. At this stage, its movements are not so quick that ultra-fast shutter speeds are called for, and as a rule, it is easier to handle than a fully grown cat. It is also very small when you sight it through the viewfinder, occupying only a small portion of the picture area, so a supplementary or long-focus lens will be helpful. Close viewpoints are essential—don't try to handle everything by yourself, have someone on hand to help you, and if there is more than one animal to deal with, have more than one helper!

The logical place to get your pictures is in the garden. If the kitten is sleeping on a chair, it isn't difficult to lift the chair slowly and steadily outside; if this is not practicable, place another chair in readiness and carry out cushion and kitten. You now stand a good chance of getting a series of pictures as it awakens, stretches itself, yawns and starts playing with that length of string held by your assistant. Tell your helper in advance what you plan to do, and where you want him or her to stand so as to be out of the field of view; this leaves you to concentrate on the camera and the actual taking. A sudden movement, an unusual noise, will generally cause the animal to look in the direction you wish, but this trick may work only once. Please don't tie on bows of ribbon; no kitten *enjoys* it.

It is folly to place a tabby on a highly-patterned cushion that will clash with the animals' markings; the background is most important, plain colours that afford good contrast should be selected. A second cushion or drape (a plain towel will do) will be required to cover the back of the chair, and it is a good idea to cover the sides too. In order that the kitten shall look small and helpless, try to include something such as a cotton-reel to create size-contrast. Don't place the chair so that shadows from tree-branches, fences or trellis-work fall across it; side-lighting will emphasize texture.

Always keep the camera down to the animal's level and work quickly, focusing accurately on the eyes. Remember that *movement close* to the camera needs faster shutter speeds to stop it than does the same movement at a greater distance.

Setting

A better plan is to use an old garden table, and go to some pains to devise a background by tacking strips of wood goal-post fashion at the rear, and stretching a plain cloth on it. Make sure this set-up stands firmly, and avoid folds and creases. Now you have a useful 'stage' which can easily be moved around to make the most of the lighting, and permits much more scope. Sleeping animals can be photographed at shutter speeds as slow as 1/30 or 1/25 sec.; waking movements require 1/100 sec. or faster, while playful actions demand the fastest speeds that conditions allow.

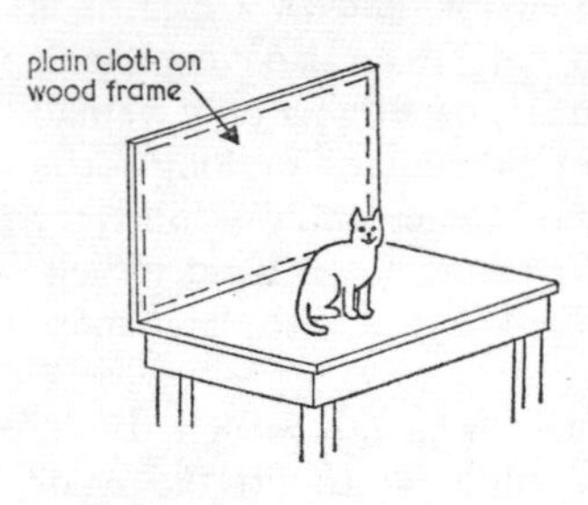

Cats

Cats have a will of their own, and if they have made up their minds not to co-operate, it is useless to continue. You cannot *make* a cat do anything. If it sits on the fence or wall in a certain place, you may be able to get a picture there with a well-filtered sky background. Try the old trick of giving it a saucer of milk, then photographing the washing attitudes that usually follow, with shutter speeds of 1/100 or 1/250 sec. if possible.

Make the most of the cat's trait of curiosity: smear a little fishpaste inside a cardboard box or container with a loose lid

Above. An exposure meter needs to be used intelligently, or prevailing conditions may over-influence its readings (see 'Using a meter' p 20). For example: with a figure standing against a background of sea and sky (top right) a reading from the camera viewpoint would include too much of the light tone, thus indicating too much stopping-down of the lens, and the subject-proper would be under-exposed. Conversely a subject against a *dark* background (top left) would be over-exposed.

Below. On the beach, it pays to keep a ready trigger-finger if you want to catch agile youngsters at play. Low viewpoints are often best—and be prepared to paddle!

Pictures of children have wide appeal. To cope with their movements, fast shutter speeds should be used. Avoid posed attitudes—give them something interesting to do, and be ready to shoot without having to make last-minute adjustments to your camera.

Pictures taken with colour film on dull, sunless days, will tend to have a cold bluish tinge. When using black-and-white film in similar conditions, better results are often obtained by slightly increasing the development time.

Pictures of trees in Autumn are usually more successful if you choose those of the larger-leafed variety (lime, chestnut, plane etc.) because small leaves are apt to look 'bitty' and scattered. The low-angle lighting needs careful handling, especially in back-lit subjects, when stray rays of light may set up lens flare.

Left. Side-lighting is excellent for revealing texture, and it produces long, interesting shadows when falling at low angles (see 'Lighting angle, p. 17).

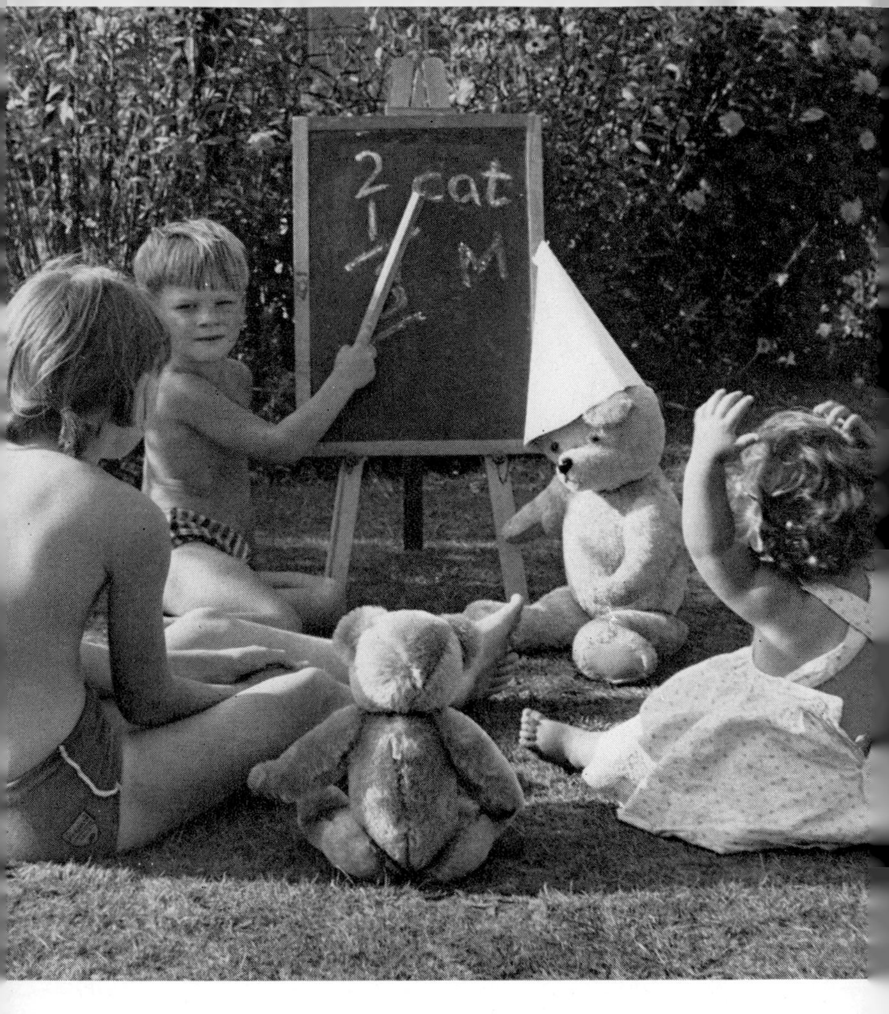

Competition pictures involving human interest should preferably 'tell a story' or depict strong character. Simple, bold appeal is more likely to succeed than attempts to crowd in too much. Lighting must be good, and print-quality first class.

Right. In colour or black-and-white, outdoor pictures at night are well worth while. By making exposures before it is completely dark, buildings, trees etc. are outlined against the sky. (see page 51).

Effective 'low-key' studies can be made by having a single photoflood lamp as the sole light source. Its placing in relation to the subject also affords helpful experience in the art of lighting.

exploit its playfulness with a ball (fast camera action here!). A sibilant 'hiss' can draw attention when needed. With a white cloth or card reflector to throw light into the shadows, get shots in back-lighting or oblique back-lighting conditions, preferably against a darkly-shadowed background. Keep an eye on that tail; a sudden twitch will produce a blur. If the cat is end-on to the camera, beware of a too-close approach which may result in distortion.

Puppies

An active puppy is seldom in one place for more than a few seconds, and only fast shutter speeds are likely to cope with the situation(s). It is better to employ catch-as-catch-can methods rather than attempt contrived set-ups, or else get your helper to hold the animal at arm's length in the air, thus giving you a sky background. A tug-of-war with an old slipper or cloth may keep the pup momentarily static in an interesting pose; alternatively, as with kittens, if all else fails—wait until he is sleepy or taking nourishment.

Young puppies can sometimes be contained in a basket or box, with heads and paws over the edge; a large bone can bring amusing attitudes.

Dogs

In most cases, dogs can be relied upon to obey commands, and are amenable to handling. Even so, a shutter speed of 1/100th. sec. or faster should be used. Lighting, background and general taking conditions should be similar to those for cats, and only one helper—preferably his master—should be needed. Surrounding a dog with onlookers is to encourage excitement and unrest; an urgent cry of 'look' or 'cats' will bring an alert stance at the right moment, constant repetition will defeat its own ends.

Head-and-shoulders pictures can be more effective than ones that show *all* the dog, and full-face is not so attractive as three-quarter face or profile as a rule; the long-focus lens is ideal for this. Keep backgrounds out of focus whenever you can, and bear in mind that it is often easier to photograph a sitting dog than a standing one. Again, avoid the too-close approach, especially with long-nosed dogs such as collies, because focusing on the eyes may mean that the nostrils are just outside the depth-of-field, and so will not be sharply rendered. Aperture and taking distance must always be adjusted to prevent this happening.

Indoor pictures

Using the fastest film, pictures by daylight indoors are possible. The strip of sunlight which falls on your carpet becomes a spotlight that can be used to good advantage. Remove any chairs etc. which appear in the background, and watch out for patches of reflected light from polished furniture. Shadows from curtaining and window frames can be a snag, but their effect can be lessened by judicious use of a photoflood lamp (when using black-and-white film). For best effect, the camera needs to be almost at floor level.

On dull days indoors, try two or more photofloods, but don't let the flex dangle around too much! The easiest way though, is to use electronic flash, you can then fire away happily at any pose or action that develops—puppies, kittens cats—all can be captured at play. Some of the finest animal studies have been achieved through electronic flash technique, and if you intend to do much animal photography it will pay you to invest in suitable equipment.

• • •

TIPS FOR CHRISTMAS PICTURES

EVERYONE LIKES TO USE their camera at Christmastime; the miniature camera in particular is pre-eminently suitable for picture-making by available light for 'human' studies, and for working in the comparatively restricted conditions of the average living rooms. What to take? Certain subjects are naturally associated with the festive season, and here are a few you might like to try. It pays to take a little trouble beforehand; whether you are using colour or monochrome film, attention to detail brings rewarding results.

Christmas trees

The lighted Christmas tree is a popular subject, but those coloured lights are deceptive! Collectively, their actinic value is low, and fairly long exposures are needed (about 1/8th. to 1/15th. sec. at *f*/3.5 with fast film) according to the number of light-coloured bulbs; reds and deep-coloured ones are less helpful. A plain background is advisable, otherwise the outline of the tree becomes lost. Keep furniture out of the picture if you can—chair-backs have a nasty habit of butting in at the wrong places. Arrange several packaged gifts and a cracker or two at the base of the tree, and introduce a child to add interest and give 'scale' to the whole thing. If the tree is large, concentrate on a chosen part of it, with the child standing close.

A normal flash shot will 'kill' the coloured lights, so if you want to use flash, try it this way: stop the lens well down (*f*/8 or smaller), put the shutter on 'B' setting, wrap two thicknesses of white handerkerchief over the flashbulb in its reflector, and keep the shutter open for a fraction of a second after it has fired the bulb. For slow colour film, the shutter should be kept open for about a second after firing the bulb. As an alternative arrangement, you can use bounced flash technique if you wish, directing the flash on to the ceiling, *without making any exposure increase* for the extra flash-to-subject distance involved.

Candle-light

Very effective shots can be made by candle-light, either as the sole light source or in conjunction with other lighting. As a working guide to exposures, it is as well to know that an ordinary domestic electric bulb gives roughly one candle-power for every watt of electricity it consumes; so a candle placed 1ft. away from a subject provides the same illumination as would a 100-watt bulb 10ft. away. With ultra-fast film therefore, exposures may be in the region of 1/30th. sec. at *f*/2.8 or *f*/3.5, while for High-speed Ektachrome for example, this becomes approximately ½ to 1 sec. at similar apertures.

For real 'Christmas card' effect, seat your model at a table close to a candelabrum with two or more lighted candles, near to a window or plain dark curtaining. Put your camera on a tripod to guard against camera shake, and remember that the subject's breath (or stray draughts) can spoil the flame shapes by flicker if the exposure is at all lengthy. Or you can direct a photoflood lamp towards the ceiling for overall shadowless illumination, ignore the candle-light for exposure purposes—base your calculations on the distance of the lamp from the ceiling plus ceiling to subject, then open up one stop more. This method is useful when you are using fast or medium-fast film, and gives a less 'yellow' result with colour film.

In every instance, the candle flame will appear insignificant unless you get as close as possible. This may call for close-up or long-focus lenses. Bear in mind that depth-of-field may be comparatively shallow, so it is best to place candle and subject more or less in the same plane when you can.

Ghosts

Why not have fun and try your hand at 'ghost' pictures? There are two ways of faking these, both involve double exposures. You can either make two separate negatives, one of the scene and another of the 'ghost' against a dark background and print them together in the enlarger; or you can make two exposures on the one frame of film (this is necessary when using colour film). Most 35mm. cameras have film transport levers interlocked with the shutter mechanism to prevent double exposures, but by disengaging the sprockets by pressing the reverse button while you operate the rapid wind lever or knob, the shutter can be tensioned without moving the film. However, sometimes a little movement does occur, and to make sure, it is better to open the camera back in complete darkness after the first exposure, and *hold* the film while you work the lever and reverse button.

Dress your 'ghost' to suit the part, and give only one-quarter of the correct exposure when photographing him in the second shot. For the best results, keep the ghost against the darkest background—matt black curtaining material is ideal. When using colour film, the effect is heightened if you use tinted lighting for the ghost (second exposure) and normal lighting for the scene. A little trial-and-error process may be needed.

Parties

Christmas parties are 'natural' subjects, and for colour shots, flash is essential. Electronic flash will catch any action; it is thus especially suitable for photographing party games, romping children etc. If you load up with ultra-fast black-and-white film, ordinary room lighting may allow exposures of 1/60 sec. at *f*/3.5 or 1/100 sec. at *f*/2.8. By putting one or more photoflood bulbs in positions where they cannot shine into the lens, even shorter exposures are possible.

Children seated round the table can be taken by having one flashbulb mounted on the camera; this is more effective in colour though, because such lighting is rather flat. If you work without flash, you also sacrifice the great depth-of-field it confers through the smaller lens apertures, consequently focusing must be accurate, and this is not always easy at a boisterous get-together. Posed 'games' and attitudes won't come off unless you are very lucky—or your actors very skilful. Most party games are repetitive, and by careful observation and judgment you can sometimes catch the vital moments and reactions with relatively slow shutter speeds such as 1/100 or 1/125 sec. Focus on the appropriate spot first, then wait with ready trigger finger.

Perhaps the biggest difficulty is that of people getting in the way unexpectedly; this is a chance you have to take if you want spontaneous expressions. For a 'different' shot which never fails to amuse the victims, get several children (or adults!) to lie on the floor fan-wise in front of you, so that all their heads are near to your feet; a straight-down shot is then taken. To increase the taking-distance you can stand on a stool or table. Alternatively, you can reverse things—put the camera on the floor and let them form a circle round it and bend over to look into the lens. This needs electronic flash; ordinary flashbulbs are disconcerting at close quarters.

Always watch the background; it can make or mar your pictures. Things such as paper chains, streamers and balloons can (and often should) be included, but hard outlines of furniture, dismembered arms and legs of guests, are *not* wanted. Unless you have to, don't try to get everyone in at once; simplicity still scores.

Lamplight

The old-fashioned oil lamp gives a wonderfully soft lighting for Christmas pictures. It imparts 'atmosphere' and quality similar to that of candle-light. If you use one for colour shots, you must include the actual lamp in the picture otherwise the yellowness of the light may be unacceptable to the viewers when the transparency is projected. If you wish, you can use bounced flash to increase the illumination, or direct a photoflood lamp towards the ceiling, but by doing so you lose much of the charm of the lamplight.

An oil lamp with a standard ½in. wick, standing say 3–4ft. from the subject, would require an exposure of approximately 1/30 sec. at *f*/3.5 with fast (400 ASA) monochrome film, 1/8 or 1/10 sec. at *f*/3.5 with High Speed Extachrome. To lighten the shadows (but beware of secondary cast shadows) ordinary candles may be strategically placed so as not to appear in the picture—their light quality will blend in. With care, you can successfully 'cheat' by arranging a 60- or 100-watt domestic lamp immediately behind the lamphouse glass, preferably with the oil lamp alight.

Christmas windows

At this time of the year, big stores go to great lengths to produce attractive and gaily-lit window displays, and you can get interesting pictures both in colour and monochrome. Either daylight or artificial-light type colour film may be used; with the slower kinds, a tripod will probably be required—and a companion to help prevent passers-by accidently kicking the tripod legs. Remember too, to take a small pocket-torch with you, to enable camera adjustments to be made in comfort!

Exposures will vary considerably; a well-lit window may need 1/8 or 1/10 sec. at *f*/6.3 with 400 ASA film. It is always best to make more than one shot, opening up and/or closing down the lens one stop. Keep an eye on the people window-shopping, especially the children with their eager faces pressed against the glass. Photographing windows in daylight presents reflection problems that often cannot be overcome without a polarizing filter, unless you hold the camera against the glass and content yourself with close-ups of selected parts of the display. Bright reflections have been known to set up lens flare, and of course, they will blot out parts of the interesting items in the shop window.

• • •

MAKING CHRISTMAS CARDS AND CALENDARS

PERSONALLY-PRODUCED Christmas cards and calendars, provided they are carefully and tastefully executed, are usually more appreciated than the ordinary ones bought over the counter, and the keen amateur can have many enjoyable evenings designing and preparing his own to send to relatives and friends. You will save yourself disappointments if you go about it systematically and work to a definite plan; the haphazard 'try this, try that' approach can only result in lack of uniformity.

Choice of subject is almost unlimited. Nowadays the wintry scene is more the exception than the rule, and summer landscapes, children, pets, still-life, are all acceptable. Bear in mind envelope proportions and sizes when you rough out your prototype card, and try to plan things so that the bromide paper is economically cut too. If you want to do things the easy way, you can of course buy Christmas folders so designed that you merely slip your print inside, but most of these suggest the 'snapshot' effort rather than a personal production.

Lettering

Apart from layout and style, the chief thing to watch is the lettering, which is the stumbling-block with most home-produced cards. It is far better to content yourself with the single word 'Greetings' nicely lettered, than to attempt ambitious 'arty' words. Squiggles, scrawls and meaningless shapes are *not* wanted; aim for simple balance. If you have a flair for hand-lettering, all is well, otherwise you must decide whether you will copy the wording from a printed card or use some form of lettering aid. 'Uno' stencils, excellent as they are, are inclined to be too formal and business-like. For tip-top results that cannot be distinguished from printer's type (because it *is* printer's type in transfer form), the 'Letraset' system is probably unbeatable.

In any event, hand-lettering each individual card is rather trying if you have a large number to prepare. To get that 'printed' look, make a sizeable enlargement of your selected picture and mount it on white card, add your lettering, then photograph the whole by means of a supplementary lens. Use slow or medium-speed film, and give slightly increased development to get more bite and contrast; with the resultant negative you can then print off as many as you wish, quickly, and with complete uniformity. Make sure that illumination is even when you copy the original, and don't over-expose, or you'll end up with a rather dense negative.

Deckle-edge trim

Naturally, double-weight bromide paper is a 'must'. Stipple or Royal surfaces look very effective, and usually a deckle-edge trim is more in keeping with the occasion. If you still prefer to print each card separately and add the wording, you may find it helpful to cut a card mask to provide a 'window' during printing, thus automatically giving pre-determined shapes, borders etc. The actual picture need not necessarily be a hard rectangle, the corners may be rounded by cutting the mask accordingly. It is all too easy to overdo this sort of thing, though.

Going back to that lettering again: you can trace printed wording on ordinary tracing paper, using a B or HB pencil; transfer it to your card, and then go over it with a pen. Alternatively, have a few trial runs with a one-stroke lettering nib on scrap paper; draw two guide lines in pencil first, then when you feel confident, tackle the card. Prints on white paper will take black or sepia drawing ink, those on cream-base paper need sepia ink only. Be prepared to spoil a card or two, so print a few more than you actually require.

There is always a great temptation to decorate cards with such things as wavy lines, miniature figures, or drawings of holly sprays, but this is dangerous unless you have natural talent in this direction. It is far wiser to play safe and let the photographic print tell the story.

Calendars

Prints for calendars have something in common with those suitable for cards: they need to be bold and simple in theme. Subjects full of fussy detail, or too many pearly grey tones without strong contrasts, have less impact and attraction. Consequently it will be found that close-up and semi-close-up studies can be used more successfully than panoramic open landscapes as a rule. Be careful too, of those pictures of junior and the family. They may be near and dear to you and yours, but not really the sort of thing to circulate as a wall calendar for your friends.

Many of the ready-prepared calendar mounts which are obtainable are most effective, both in paste-on and slip-in form, so if do-it-yourself does not greatly appeal, you can use these with every confidence. For those who prefer to start from scratch, calendar-making can prove a most satisfying and enjoyable procedure. It does not take long, even if you hand-letter the word 'calendar', and it gives you *carte blanche* regarding size and shape. Once again, decorative symbols and shapes are 'out', and so are bizarre, stunty treatments. A good print, a pleasing subject, neat assembly—and you can't go wrong.

The standard plain 'Club' type mounts with white/cream facings are convenient and suitable. A wholeplate print (upright) goes well on a 10 x 8in. mount, a 10 x 8in. print on a 12 x 10in. mount and so on, leaving a satisfactory broad border at the base for good balance. This border needs to be considerably wider if you intend to stick the calendar tab on to the mount itself; generally it looks better hanging below, leaving the mounted print isolated. Print-mounting should be carried out in your usual way, by dry-mounting, rubber-gum, or rapid mounting solution. Paste is not recommended, owing to its tendency to make the mount curl when drying.

Attractive combination

Deckle-edge prints are less formal than straight-bordered ones; in fact, it's better to trim the border off altogether if you have not got a deckle-edge trimmer, and draw a pencil line border on the mount about ⅛ to ¼in. away from the print edge after mounting, using a soft B or BB pencil. When mounting deckle-edge prints, do not carry the adhesive right to the edges—the 'loose' effect is more pleasing. Remember to put cream prints on the cream side of the mount, and vice versa, and get matching calendar tabs.

The materials you will need are: tinsel (or ordinary) ribbon ¼in. wide; adhesive (or gummed) tape ½in. wide, calendar insets and tabs. All these are obtainable from good stationers. An attractive combination is achieved with gold tinsel and gold metal foil gummed strip for use with cream mounts, and silver or grey with white. Beware of vivid, brightly coloured ribbons or tapes, as these will tend to be more eye-catching than your picture. If you are mounting a colour print for use as a calendar, try to select ribbon that matches or nearly matches some dominant colour in the picture.

The method of construction is shown in the illustrations on page 148. There is nothing difficult or complicated about it, but remember to do the job properly. For instance, measure up the centres for accurate hanging and placing of the tab, otherwise it may be unbalanced and off-centre when you turn your handiwork round frontwards. Don't hang the tab *too* low, between $\frac{1}{4}$ to $\frac{3}{4}$in. from the bottom of the mount is generally about right. It *must* hang parallel to the base of the mount, the smallest error here will give a lop-sided appearance to the whole thing. The ribbon should be equidistant from the sides of the tab and about $\frac{1}{2}$in. from the edges. Attention to these details makes all the difference to a really worthwhile and presentable job. As a finishing touch, the calendar may be wrapped in clear cellophane fastened with transparent sticky tape; or you may like to wrap it in white tissue instead . . . *never* brown paper.

• • •

FIFTY DARKROOM TIPS

1 With some tanks, there is a tendency for the end of the film to creep out of the spiral reel during development, especially when the tank is designed for rotational agitation. To prevent this, cut a small flat wedge of rubber, and push it into the groove after loading the film, so that it firmly anchors the end in place. Naturally, this must be done in total darkness. Alternatively, the wedge may be positioned immediately behind the end of the film, to form a stop in the groove at this

point. Two such wedges (one in the top and the other in the bottom) may be used with roll film if desired, for extra safety.

2 *If your enlarging lens is one of those which has to be stopped down on the* face *of the lens mount (as opposed to the present-day practice of engraving the figures round the rim), hold a white card or mirror underneath with the enlarger switched on, so that light is reflected back onto the figures.*

3 By working with the enlarger lens at full aperture, a slight softness in definition may result. This can be useful in the case of portraits for instance. Should exposure time become too brief, it can be increased by putting a yellow filter on the lens. Softening definition by simply deliberately throwing the lens slightly out-of-focus is inadvisable, and usually unacceptable.

4 *The vapour given off by acid-hardener fixer can be harmful to any metal objects nearby, so keep your enlarger properly covered when not in use. It often pays to smear a trace of vaseline on all bright metal parts, not only to prevent rust forming, but also to hold any dust particles which settle and may otherwise float onto the bromide paper during lengthy exposures as the lamphouse sets up warm air currents.*

5 Documents, drawings, photographs etc. can be copied by means of the enlarger. First, position the drawing on the enlarging board, place a negative in the carrier and adjust the projected image to cover the area; focus accurately, stop down the lens. Remove the negative, and in complete darkness replace it with a cut length of film. Carefully wrap the enlarger lamphouse in lightproof cloth so that only the lens is left uncovered, then illuminate the drawing you wish to copy. Fairly even lighting is often achieved by using a single light source and moving it all round the area. Exposure time depends upon the amount of stopping down, speed of negative material, amount of light and the area it covers—trial exposures are generally necessary. Don't make the mistake of switching on the enlarger lamp instead!

6 *Even if you have a white-based masking (or printing) frame upon which to project your negatives for focusing and picture-composing, it is best to insert a piece of paper the same thickness as that you intend to print on (the back of a scrap print will do admirably). This ensures that when you focus for maximum sharpness, the image will be in the same plane as the surface of your bromide paper.*

7 When making big enlargements with the lamphouse nearly as high as it will go, make sure that the edge of the image does not fall on the highly polished metal column, or it will reflect light which may affect the bromide paper. Wrap a dark cloth, duster, or black paper round the base of the upright.

8 *From time to time, the enlarger lamphouse should be dismantled, the lamp removed and washed in warm soapy water, and the condensers and lens taken out. These should be carefully cleaned with lens-cleaning fluid or water to which a little wetting-agent has been added. Coated lenses should only be lightly brushed over with a soft brush, or treated according to the maker's instructions. Make sure your hands are clean and dry, in case you inadvertently touch the surface of the optical glass. Check over all screws and fittings to see that nothing is loose.*

9 When specks of dust form on the surface of the enlarger condenser, do not remove them by rubbing with silk or similar material, as this electrifies the glass and causes it to attract the particles even more. Instead, paste a strip of soft chamois leather onto a small flat stick or piece of thick card, and use this to gently wipe over the condenser face. Keep the 'wiper' in a box or polythene bag, away from dirt and dust, and renew it when necessary.

10 *Your darkroom dishes should be used for one specific purpose only, to prevent possible contamination by left-over traces of chemicals. To make sure mistakes will not occur, mark each dish on one side by painting the appropriate initial letter 'D', 'S' and 'F' for developer, stop-bath and fixer respectively,*

using coloured nail varnish. You will find that the polish is durable, and easily renewed when required.

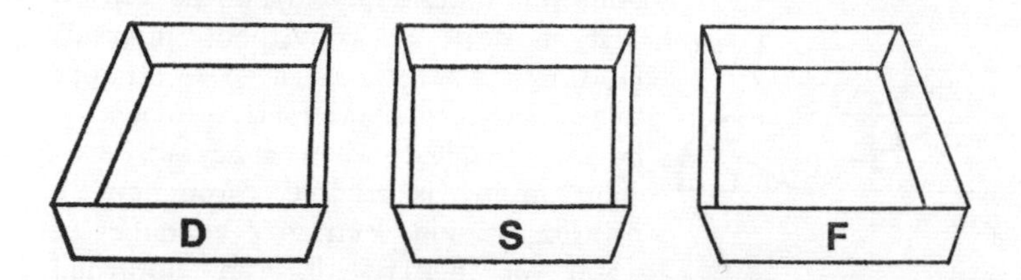

11 In an emergency, you can dry a washed print in eight or ten minutes. Blot it thoroughly, then place between two dry blotters and 'iron' with a domestic iron (the heat control turned to 'low'), changing the blotters if necessary. Naturally, fluffless blotting-paper must be used; for glossies, put the prints on a glazing plate, cover with blotter and apply the heated iron.

12 *Developing tanks, even when stored in cupboards, usually collect dust through the lid openings. Prevent this by keeping them in polythene bags; do the same for your film wiper, sponge etc.—it pays dividends!*

13 An old-fashioned chest of drawers can be most useful in the darkroom. Solid and firm, it makes an excellent working-top on which to stand the enlarger; one about 36in. high will be found to be ideal. The drawers provide plenty of accommodation for boxes of paper etc., and if desired, can be partitioned to file away numbered negatives conveniently. A well-made chest will allow bromide paper to be left unwrapped in a drawer during a printing session, without risk of fogging.

14 *Keep a roll of kitchen paper on your darkroom wall. It is useful for mopping up spilt liquids, drying your hands etc., and has the virtue that it does not leave stray fibres in the same way that cloth does.*

15 Exposure times for making test strips and enlarging can be accurately assessed and repeated simply by counting the drips from an ordinary domestic water tap. Adjust the tap so that it drips at convenient intervals (audibly). There is no need to attempt to get one-second intervals; provided it is not touched when once set, constant timing is assured throughout a printing session. Putting a container of water—or better still, an upturned empty tin—under the dripping tap increases the noise of the 'plop'.

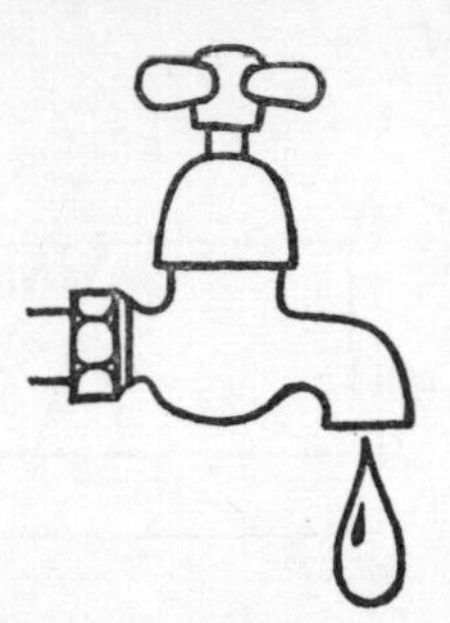

16 *Lime scum from the wash water may dry into the surface of your prints. It is difficult to remove when dry, so always wipe over each print with a clean sponge before drying and/or glazing. This also removes excess water, speeds drying, and lets blotters deal with more prints before becoming saturated.*

17 Many darkroom scales have pans which will not hold more than an ounce or two at a time. Some chemicals, such as sodium carbonate, are used in formulae requiring several ounces. Waxed paper cups (or thin plastic ones) will solve the problem—put one on each pan of the scale for balance. The waxed surface allows re-use.

18 *A foot-switch is a worth-while buy. It leaves your hands free for dodging and 'burning-in' during enlarging. Better still—invest in an enlarger time switch.*

19 When pouring liquids into a bottle from a container or jar that has no pouring lip, place a glass stirring rod across the top of the container and hold it in place with the forefinger. Pour carefully, and the liquid will flow along the rod into the bottle.

20 *Avoid using old, stale bromide paper for your normal work; keep it for proofing and unimportant record prints. If you have*

to use suspect paper, always add some restrainer (such as Johnson's '142') to the working solution to minimize staining whenever 'forcing' becomes necessary. Store paper where temperature and humidity are moderate.

21 Raised figures on transparent measures can be made more readable by coating them with dark lacquer. An additional coat of clear lacquer gives extra protection.

22 *The swab you keep for general use in the darkroom should be thoroughly washed each time, to avoid chemical or fibrous traces being left on bottle mouths etc.*

23 Never use a ball-point pen to number the backs of your prints when developing. There is a risk of the ink being transferred to print surfaces while the paper is wet.

24 *Film tank reels can be speedily dried when necessary by brushing out excess water with a clean paint brush, the remaining moisture then being removed by standing the reel some distance from the front of a blower fire (low heat) or other source of moderate warmth. Remember to use that brush again when dry, to get rid of any dust particles which may have been blown into the grooves.*

25 If your masking frame is inclined to slip on the enlarger baseboard, small pieces of *cloth* surgical tape on the underside will provide a grip. One piece near each corner and in the centre should suffice. Alternatively, cover the base (or the enlarger baseboard) with thin sheet cork.

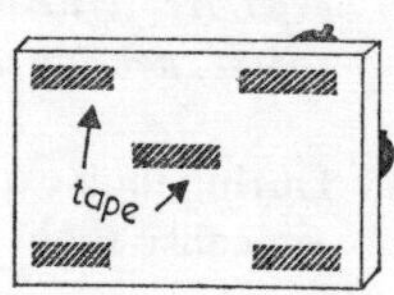

26 *It is false economy to overwork the fixer, either with films or paper. Remember too, that below 60° F fixing solutions cannot work properly.*

27 Before re-using any narrow-mouthed bottle, it should be cleaned with a small bottle brush. Simply filling with water,

shaking and rinsing, will not always remove deposits in the neck.

28 *Single-weight bromide paper may fog slightly during lengthy exposures, due to light passing through the paper and being reflected back from the white face of the masking board. A piece of black paper placed underneath (before adjusting focus) will overcome this, and thereby improve contrast.*

29 Labels on bottles will last longer if they are covered with transparent Sellotape.

30 *Don't dust your darkroom immediately before loading films or printing; if you have to, then wait until airborne particles settle before working. Never neglect to dust (or vacuum-clean) regularly.*

31 A test-strip that has not been allowed to develop *fully* before fixing is an unreliable guide. Never hasten the development of test-strips, nor make them on bromide paper of similar grade but from a different batch. The same applies to paper surface—a test-strip should not be made on glossy (for instance) if the print itself is to be on semi-matt or 'Royal'.

32 *Signatures, or any titling, can be added to a print by means of an old fountain pen filled with hypo solution. Before making the exposure, write on an area which will print dark; let it dry, then expose, develop and fix in the normal way.*

33 During long exposures, do not walk about the darkroom. This can cause slight vibration and so affect definition.

34 *In hard water districts it is advisable to give films a final rinse in a 2% solution of acetic acid before hanging to dry, to prevent the formation of whitish deposits. The* celluloid *side of 35mm. films may be wiped dry with damp chamois or a soft handkerchief if desired. Avoid touching the emulsion. Many workers use a proprietary film wiper to good effect.*

35 Negatives and negative-carriers etc. can be kept free of dust

by applying a little anti-static solution. It can also be used for transparencies, cover glasses and plastic frames when preparing slides, but is not recommended for the treatment of lenses.

36 *New interest can sometimes be given to pictures simply by reversing the negatives in the enlarger carrier. Compositions which 'read' from left to right are usually best. Obviously negatives of well-known scenes, buildings, portraits etc. cannot be reversed; but many subjects* can, *and gain pictorially by this.*

37 Miniature negatives should never be stored in roll form, as winding and unwinding them gives rise to scratches, and encourages 'clock spring' tendencies that make handling difficult. Store in strips of four or six in suitable wallets or folders. Home-made folders of ordinary paper are seldom entirely free of residual chemicals which may do harm.

38 *Never clean glazing plates with proprietary detergents. Most of these products contain small quantities of sodium silicate, which can cause prints to stick to the surface of the plate. Silver polish such as* Silvo *is very suitable.*

39 When trimming the leading end of 35mm. film from bulk stock, or cutting a short length, try to avoid cutting *through*

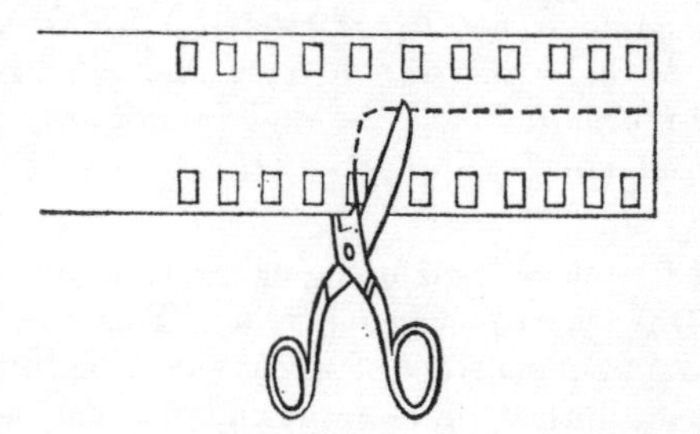

perforations, otherwise tearing may occur at this point. This is particularly so in the case of a Leica 'tongue'.

40 *White or light-coloured clothing worn while printing can reflect light from the projected image; and during long exposures may cause slight loss of print brilliance. Similarly, reflected light from nearby walls can be troublesome. Wear dark clothing if possible, and put black paper near the enlarger if the walls are white or light-toned.*

41 The popular expanded polystyrene ceiling tiles make useful mats upon which to stand dishes and/or your developing tank. Their insulating properties help to prevent heat loss through the base during cold weather.

42 *Even when used with care, viscose sponges used for wiping down prints or films can retain hard-to-remove dirt. When this happens, let the sponge dry until quite hard, then slice off the surface(s) with a sharp knife.*

43 If you haven't an enlarger cover, slip a large polythene bag over it. Some bags (sold to hold soiled linen) are complete with draw-string. Cloth covers are apt to leave fibrous traces which may cling to negative carriers etc.

44 *To minimize grain when enlarging from a grainy negative, put a diffusion (soft focus) disc on the enlarger lens, or diffuse the projected image with crumpled cellophane, old nylon stocking etc. The disc may be used for only* part *of the full exposure time when the grain is not too assertive, in which case it can be simply held under the lens for easy and quick removal. Contrasts and definition will be slightly softened, with shadows being spread into the highlights a little.*

45 Well-used reels of developing tanks tend to cause films to stick in the grooves when loading. This can generally be cured by applying a trace of silicone-bearing furniture polish, using a soft, lintless cloth on the end of a matchstick, running along each groove. Polish in a similar manner, or brush well with a soft brush. Make sure that no excess polish is allowed to remain.

46 *When washing films, remove the lid of the tank and insert a funnel in the centre column of the reel. Water now flows direct to the bottom of the tank, and rinses through the reel, thus preventing fixer from settling in the base of the tank.*

47 Before using a new chromium glazing plate for the first time, it is advisable to wash it well with soap and water, taking care not to scratch the surface. Excessive zeal in polishing may do more harm than good, especially if a coarse cloth is used.

48 *Photographic chemicals, whether in solid or liquid form, should not be stored in a hot place. Conversely, although solid chemicals are generally unaffected by cold, concentrated solutions should not be stored at temperatures below 45°F.*

49 If you use self-adhesive tape to fasten 35mm. film to a cassette spindle, take care not to pull it off hastily when loading the film into a tank in the darkroom. Torn quickly from the film, it can sometimes produce a luminous effect, and in dry conditions, even create a tiny spark. Normally this may not affect the film, but with ultra-fast emulsions it is possible for the static discharge to produce markings on the last few frames.

50 *A simple way to test the efficiency of your enlarging lens is to fog a piece of film, and scratch lines on it with a point of a needle. Using a fairly hard grade of bromide paper, make enlargements from this 'scratch-neg'. working first at full aperture, then at the stop(s) you normally use. Don't confine the scratched lines to the centre: make sure the corners of the print have their quota of lines, and check particularly the rough edges of the enlarged scratches, for there the fine detail is more in evidence. Alternatively of course, you can buy a line test negative produced specially for the purpose; these are often sold as 'focusing negatives'.*

• • •

HINTS ON ENLARGING

WHILE IT IS TRUE that many satisfactory enlargements can be made by straightforward printing, it is a fact that a higher standard of printing technique—and therefore better results—can be obtained by effective local control and manipulation. Since a negative might have a tonal range in the order of 250:1, and the maximum tonal range that could be expected from a glossy print is in the region of 50:1, it is obvious that some form of judicious adjustment or tone-balance during printing should improve matters, by preventing certain parts darkening too much, and/or others remaining too light.

The most commonly-used methods consist of 'shading and dodging', burning-in, and water-bath development; but no amount of juggling and control will produce first-class results from a poor negative, although it may make a print acceptable. Shading is usually carried out by holding a piece of card between the bromide paper and the enlarger lens, thus masking the rays of light in the area immediately below, Big, small, and quite intricate areas can be controlled, and kept lighter in tone by means of a few simple shapes of thin card threaded on to lengths of wire. Some prefer to use a piece of Plasticine instead of card, because it can be instantly squeezed into any desired shape; others make use of cotton wool, especially when shading clouds in a picture.

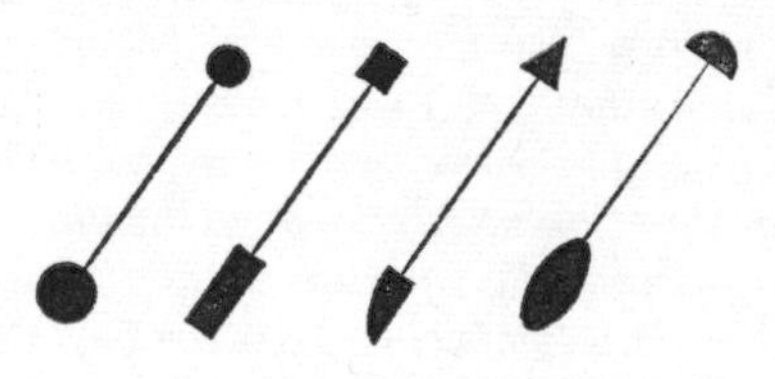

It is a good plan to make several of these little 'dodgers' as they are called, varying them in size and shape, keeping a spare wire handy so that any special shape which may be needed can be cut and threaded on to the wire straight away. Increasing the distance of the dodger from the paper increases the area if shades, and softens the edges of the shadow it forms. However, it is unwise to hold it further away than about one-third of the distance from paper to lens, because it then tends to affect nearby areas which are not required to be shaded. Thus it must always be nearer to the paper than to the lens; in practice, two inches above the paper is about right in most cases.

The shape and size of the shadow can be varied by tilting the dodger at different angles, but it *must* be kept constantly on the move or else its use will produce an all-too-obvious patch on the finished print. Again, unless the wire support is thin and also kept slightly moving from side to side or radially, a faint line or streak may be registered by its shadow. Some professionals use their hands and fingers to shade and 'dodge' an enlargement; considerable skill and experience is needed for this, especially when relatively small areas require treatment, or when the areas are centrally positioned.

Application

It must be remembered that local control is but a means to an end, and should never be overdone; like spotting and finishing —the better it is executed, the less it should be seen, or even suspected. By half-closing your eyes to examine the projected image on the enlarging frame (which should hold a piece of white paper the same thickness as the intended print, so that focusing will be accurate; the back of a scrap print is ideal) it is easier to decide which parts of the picture are likely to need dodging, the extra dark and extra light patches that require attention then showing more clearly.

If you have to cut a special shape, put a book or a box about two inches deep in the appropriate area, place a piece of card on top and outline the image with a pencil; now when the shape is cut out, good coverage should be achieved working at this distance. Do not re-adjust the focus when you outline the shape for cutting, nor trace it at baseboard-level.

Highlights

To bring out detail in highlights, 'burning-in' is generally resorted to, the areas concerned being given extra exposure by means of a hole in the centre of a card held (and continuously moved) in the same way as the wire dodger. The hole should be smaller than the part to be treated: it will be found that one approximately ¼in. in diameter serves effectively, as the card can be held further from the bromide paper when desired. Ordinary paper, or thin white card should not be used for this, otherwise there is a risk of light from the enlarger diffusing through it during lengthy operations, and so fogging the print. If you can obtain a red or orange-tinted sheet of celluloid, positioning of the burning-in spot of light is facilitated; this should never be attempted however without first testing the celluloid by placing it on a scrap of bromide paper. Put a coin on top, then switch on the enlarger light; if the paper shows any image of the coin after, say, 60 secs. exposure, the celluloid should not be used. Ideally, of course, it should be perfectly safe, no matter how protracted the exposure. Celluloid that is reasonably safe for bromide paper is not necessarily safe for chlorobromide papers.

Skies often require additional exposure time during printing. In some cases all that is necessary is to hold a sheet of card so that its edge roughly coincides with the skyline, and so protects the ground area from over-printing; the card distance should again be about two inches above the bromide paper. Care is needed to prevent a dark line appearing along the horizon, the card being kept moving and not allowed to let its shadow fall below the horizon. Buildings, trees etc. which break into the sky portion usually complicate matters, and again a matching shape mask should be cut.

Exposure determination

Most dodging problems can be solved by thoughtful use of test-strips; indeed, the wise photographer seldom, if ever, makes an enlargement without one. A small test piece placed in the requisite area(s) in addition to the normal test-strip, and developed fully, eliminates the guesswork. Exposure determination is particularly important when a hard grade of paper is being used, because its shortened exposure scale is more readily affected by an increase or decrease than are normal or soft grades. Shading an area for anything less than one-quarter of the exposure time given to the print is unlikely to show much improvement; in some instances an area may be shaded for sonething like one-half of the printing time. When printing up a sky, twice as much exposure may be needed, especially with a hard negative.

The *depth* of tone to which a print is carried is to a certain extent a question of personal taste—and the nature of the subject; there are those who favour rich deep blacks in abundance, while others prefer lighter effects. Occasionally a delicate high-key subject calls for light printing, but the average negative is best translated in depths between these extremes. If the print is to become a wall picture, or mounted for exhibition purposes, it should be a shade darker in tone, otherwise at normal viewing distances it will appear weak and lacking in quality.

Development

A chlorobromide print which is darkening too quickly in the developer can be whipped out and fixed without detrimental loss of quality as a rule, though it may then be warmer in tone; if this is done with ordinary bromide print, weak blacks and a muddy look results. Should the image be coming up too slowly, and there is evidence that it will be too pale, development may be forced. An increase of ten or twelve degrees in the temperature of the developer will help, and it is usually possible to give three times normal development before chemical fog sets in (the addition of a restrainer such as Johnson's 142 or similar minimizes staining and fogging). The print can be left face-down in water while the developer is warmed up.

If only a *part* of the print needs a little extra darkening after normal development, this can be done by applying undiluted developer in that area, using either a small brush or wad of cotton wool pushed into the end of a length of glass tubing. Keep a little concentrated developer handy in a container—an old cup will do; this treatment is particularly useful for strengthening the eyes in portraits, or for emphasizing any important detail in a compostion. Care must be taken to make sure that the neat developer does not run down the print when it is lifted for application, or it may cause dark streaks. Remember too, that *cold* developer should not be used.

Water-bath development

Sometimes, despite shading and dodging, shadow areas might

still tend to become too dark and thus lose detail. When this happens, marked improvement can often be effected by adopting the water-bath method of development, which reduces contrast; in fact its results may be equivalent to those obtained with a paper one grade softer, and it is therefore also useful when the paper is rather hard for the negative.

The procedure is as follows: as soon as the image starts to appear, the print is lifted from the developer and transferred face downwards without draining into a dish of water (at a temperature of 65°–70°F) and left there for about a minute, without agitation. Then it is again lifted into the developer, and when this re-commences its darkening action, the print is removed to the water as before for a similar period of time. The process is continued regularly until the image is satisfactory, then the print is rinsed and fixed. To guard against possible fogging

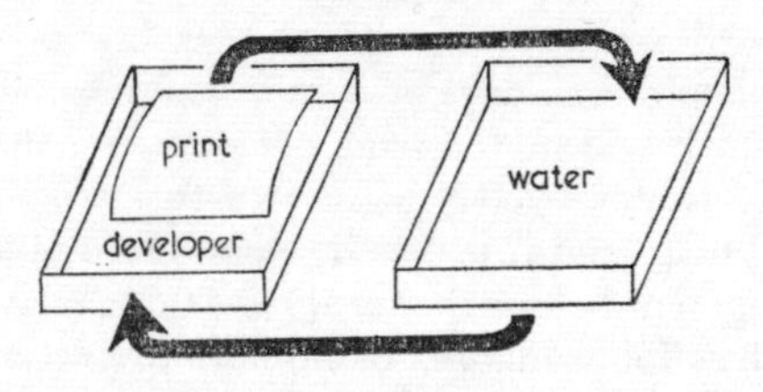

and staining during this prolonged development, a little developer improver such as Johnson's 142 can be added; in certain cases, it may be an advantage to increase the exposure time during printing.

This technique allows the highlights to develop more fully while it retards the action in the shadow portions. The developer is held in the emulsion and continues its action in the water; since it has little darkening to do in the highlight areas, it is not so quickly exhausted as it is in the shadow portions, where it soon stops working. Thus it provides a sort of automatic balancing process. The treatment is very useful for negatives of interiors which require detail in windows, open doorways with brightly-lit scenes beyond, and artificial light studies which include the light-source. It also helps to bring out cloud details in skies.

Diffusion

Pictorial subjects can at times be improved by diffusing the image when printing, and so blurring definition slightly by softening it —as opposed to unsharpness caused by incorrect focusing. Diffusion creates light-scatter, and when used in enlarging it has the effect of spreading the shadow areas into the highlights, the image having a soft appearance in consequence. (When a diffuser is used on the camera lens for photographing, light is scattered *from the highlights into the shadow areas*, producing a pleasing halation and softened contrasts).

You can buy special diffusion discs to put on the camera or enlarging lens, or you can make a diffuser from crumpled Cellophane, muslin, black chiffon, bolting silk. If preferred, the material can be stretched over a hole in a card. As a rule, printing exposure times need increasing by 40%–50% when using a fine diffuser, and whatever kind is used, approximately half the exposure should be made without diffusion; in other words, for an enlargement requiring say 20 secs. the diffuser should be brought into use after the first 10 or 12 secs. In this way, sufficient image sharpness is still retained to prevent fuzziness.

As well as softening definition, graininess is lessened, and contrast is weakened; it may therefore be desirable to make your print on a harder grade of paper. The technique must be used with discretion and taste—it does not suit all pictures. Glamour studies and portraits of girls are often diffused because of its flattering effect; in addition, less retouching is required.

• • •

HINTS ON GLAZING

THE GLAZING OF A print on glossy paper brings out all the qualities of its tonal range, and imparts a truly 'professional' finish; visual contrast is increased because the high gloss reduces the amount of light scattered by the print surface. In theory, glazing is a process that should present no difficulties, but in practice all sorts of snags seem to crop up from time to time, apparently without explanation, and many 'old hands' have various pet methods to offset these. If you haven't already done so, no doubt you will eventually evolve your own to suit your particular needs. However, certain fundamentals and basic techniques cannot be ignored; careful, clean working being the key to success.

It is as well to remember that the finished print surface will have a replica of the glazing surface, so that the more highly-polished the latter, the better will be the glaze; for this reason, polished plate glass and cold glazing produces the finest results, but takes far longer than the conventional hot glazing by hot-bed glazers. Among the materials that can be used to impart a glaze are the following: glass (plate or window), polished stainless steel, chromium-plated metal sheets, and 'Perspex'. Glass has a reputation for causing prints to stick, and must of course be placed on a perfectly flat surface when squeegeeing prints on to it, or it will break.

To prepare new plate glass for glazing, first wash well with warm soapy water, rinse and dry thoroughly with soft colth; then gently polish with french chalk moistened with methylated spirit (or 'Silvo' silver polish), dusting off the chalk when the spirit has dried. The surface of the wet print must be completely free from grit or scum, and to ensure this, swab it over with a wet hand and then give a quick rinse in clean water. Cotton wool should never be used as a swab, as loose fibres from it can stick to the emulsion of the print.

Before squeegeeing down the print, the surface of the glass should be swilled with clean water, leaving a generous pool to receive the print; plenty of water prevents air being left between print and glass after squeegeeing. A roller squeegee is preferred by many, because it is less likely to displace the prints when first applied; it also allows more pressure to be used until true optical contact with the glass surface is achieved. By inspecting the print through the other side of the glass, any remaining air-bells can be detected and dealt with. If there are any stray particles, the print should be peeled off immediately, the unwanted particles removed, and the print squeegeed down again. Moderate pressure is all that is needed as a rule.

Surplus water is then blotted off and the print allowed to dry naturally; the application of heat, especially in the early stages, can cause the print to stick—or else peel off without any glaze. By leaving prints overnight, and then gently lifting a corner to peel off, all should be well. Prints that stick are best removed by immersing the whole sheet of glass in cold water for several hours. Glazing solutions are available that greatly facilitate things, and generally prevent sticking occuring.

Double-weight papers

Due to their thickness, double-weight papers make prints difficult to glaze, and are more prone to give 'oyster-shell' marks —concentric rings created by prints coming away a little at a time from the glazing surface. When using double-weight papers intended for glazing, it is advisable to avoid a fixer-hardening bath, as this toughens the emulsion to make optical contact with the sheet more difficult.

The squeegee must be applied more heavily than with single-weight papers. This extra pressure means that glass about ¼in. thick should be used; as a safety measure, the corners and edges should be rounded off for comfortable handling, always watching that all-important surface, since even minute scratches will be reproduced on prints. Similar care must be exercised when polishing. Cold glazing *can* be carried out with metal glazing sheets too, but they are normally intended for heated print-dryers.

Metal sheets

Chromium-plated sheets generally have a better surface finish than the stainless steel, however, the surface is less durable as a rule—in time it tends to develop small pits. Both kinds may be safely polished with 'Silvo' silver polish, and when not in use, should be stored in their original envelopes and packing; never glaze directly on to a new sheet without first washing it in warm soap and water to remove possible traces of grease. To 'condition' the surface, it is as well to first glaze a batch of prints that are spares or duplicates, waste prints will do; because new glazing sheets tend to give rise to slight sticking. Subsequent batches should come away without any trouble.

Routine

The draining board at the side of the kitchen sink is as good a place as any to position the wet prints on to the wet sheets, allowing the surplus water to run into the sink without splashing on to the floor. From here, the glazing sheet can be transferred to a nearby table top or bench covered with several thicknesses of newspaper, finally squeegeeing and blotting off before placing in the heated glazer. When new, the cloth on a glazer may be somewhat hairy; this disappears after a while.

It is important to make sure the cloth is well tensioned, otherwise the prints may come away bit by bit beneath it, to cause 'oyster shell' drying marks which can only be removed by soaking and re-glazing. Also make sure that the cloth is quite dry to the touch before you release it to take out the prints; cracking noises sometimes occur during glazing, indicating that the glazing is almost completed. When the cloth is released, the prints should spring free of their own accord; premature removal leaves the middle still adhering to the glazing plate while the edges of the print have freed themselves. Replacing the cloth in such circumstances is not likely to overcome the oyster-shell marking that has formed, and in fact a print may become folded back and creased in one corner.

Allow plenty of time for prints to dry, but don't 'cook' them. If you do, cockling may occur, with the result that the prints will not lie flat. To avoid contamination for future prints, those intended for glazing must be really thoroughly washed, otherwise the cloth on the glazer will carry over hypo from batch to batch. Similarly, the cloth should be washed periodically to remove ordinary dirt. For safety, the glazer should always be 'earthed' and the mains cable itself checked from time to time to ensure no plugs have become loose or wire coverings frayed.

Glazing faults

Apart from the common faults of oyster-shell markings and prints sticking, these things can occur: grit marks—tiny pits in the gelatine with a particle of grit in the centre and no glaze; fleck marks—small or large areas without glaze, caused by imperfect contact between print and glazing sheet. This latter may be due to insufficient water when squeegeeing down, uneven pressure with squeegee, or by excessive hardening of the print emulsion in a fixer-hardener solution.

Careless cleaning of glazing plates will of course give rise to other marks and blemishes. In some areas, hard water will deposit lime on the surface which is hard to remove without risk of scratching; the cure is to fit a small filter on the domestic tap, or use filtered rain water, Suitable filters are available from photographic dealers.

• • •

HINTS ON PRINT FINISHING

Most photographers, especially those who exhibit their work, indulge in a certain amount of handwork and finishing on enlargements; and it is true to say that very often a photograph can be improved beyond all recognition by a few deft touches here and there. The secret lies in being *painstaking*—rushed, heavy-handed treatment will do more harm than good. Properly-executed handwork should not in fact be visible, at least, not from normal viewing-distances, unless it has had to be fairly extensive and 'strong'.

Knifing

Usually, a retouching knife is used for this, the idea being to lightly scrape off some of the print surface in order to remove black marks or spots, or to lighten small areas of tone. Instead of a retouching knife, try using half an old safety-razor blade of the ordinary three-slotted type. To break it, wrap it in a piece of cloth and bend sharply with forefingers and thumbs; with care, it is possible to make a diagonal break, which gives finer and sharper working edges and points. Armed with this, small dark specks, lines etc. can be removed with a minimum of surface scraping, and after practising on scrap prints it will probably be found to be superior to a retouching knife.

The work must be carried out with the lightest 'featherweight' touch, and requires practice to get the knack and to hold the blade at the correct angle to the print surface—this differs with individual workers, from almost vertical to a decided slope, but once accustomed to, the process becomes easy and certain. On no account should the point of the blade be used to 'dig' deeply, no matter how dark the spot which has to be taken out, it is fatal to try and hurry things. Discard the blade as soon as it shows signs of blunting; a really sharp edge is essential for clean working.

Although knifing can be carried out on glossy prints, it is usually detectable when the print is held at an angle; by applying a little gum (taken from ordinary paper gumstrip by means of a wet spotting-brush) the roughened area can be made less obvious, the gum imparting a sheen as it dries. Spirit varnish is sometimes used to cover knifed spots in this manner, on semi-matt as well as glossy papers. Alternatively, papers other than glossy may be treated with proprietary 'dope' that can be bought for the purpose; this also helps to darken the general tone of the print. The disadvantage with most dopes is that they tend to make the print surface slightly sticky, so that dust particles etc. adhere to it after a time.

Chemical spotting

To remove black spots and other small dark areas from glossy prints (before glazing) it is more satisfactory to bleach them away chemically. This is best done immediately the print leaves the fixing bath. Do not wash, but wipe the hypo from the print surface with cotton-wool or viscose sponge, and then touch the spot with the tip of a fine spotting brush that has been moistened with water and touched on a crystal of potassium ferricyanide. As soon as bleaching takes place, wipe over with cotton wool liberally wetted with hypo; return the print to the fixer for a minute or two, then wash and dry as usual. (Note: do not put the brush in your mouth).

If, as is usual, the ferricyanide leaves a white spot, this can be rectified by 'spotting' with dye, water colour or medium. This chemical method of reduction of tone can of course be used with matt, semi-matt, Royal-surfaced papers as well as glossy.

White spots

White spots are usually dealt with by filling-in with a series of minute dots made by very light touches with the pointed tip of a brush holding a little spotting dye, water colour or medium as

RETOUCHING TRICKS

If you find that the spotting medium or dye does not 'take' readily on the surface of a print, this is probably due to the presence of grease through handling. It can usually be remedied by touching the moist brush on a piece of soap, or better still, artists' ox gall (obtainable from most fine art dealers).

Instead of scraping out wrinkles, neck-lines and creases under the eyes in portraits, if is often better to blend them into the surrounding light tones by means of spotting medium or dye. This avoids abrasion of the print surface, and when carefully done, makes the retouching less detectable.

Much more accurate (and finer) spotting and retouching can be carried out if you work with the aid of a good magnifier.

It is generally considered best to have only one 'catch-light' in each eye in portraits, any others being spotted out. Emphasis can be given by slightly darkening the pupils, and hair high-lights accentuated by darkening the shadows *with a light wash of dye or medium.*

If too much dye is applied to a spot, making it darker than the surrounding area, it is sometimes better to lightly scrape it off to the right tone, rather than attempt to lighten it by washing. A wet finger quickly applied, will frequently remove excess dye before it can soak into the emulsion, but once it has penetrated deeply, dye needs considerable washing out.

Spotting is made easier if you use a half-dry brush with a good point; this allows fine control and more precise working.

previously stated. For efficient working, it is best to 'get the feel' of the operation by spending a few minutes with a scrap print first. When you are ready to start on the print-proper, place a sheet of white paper close to the area needing treatment, otherwise finger-marks or moisture from the hands may make it difficult for the spotting colour to 'take'.

Put a small blob of the colour or dye in a saucer, moisten the brush and then merely touch this. Gently twirling against the saucer, draw the point across the edge until the brush is free of surplus moisture and well pointed. Test for depth of tone on a piece of paper; it should be somewhat darker than that to which you have to bring your white speck, because it dries out lighter. Hold the brush fairly upright, and put the *smallest possible* spot of colour on at a time; if things go wrong, wipe over quickly with a damp rag and start again.

Retouching dye has the advantage of sinking right into the emulsion instead of lying on the surface, as water colour and medium do, so the tone can be built up without fear of removing any already deposited—which frequently happens with the other two. For the same reason, dye is less detectable, even on a glossy print; if too much is applied, it can only be removed by washing the print or by carefully scraping with the blade or knife. It is therefore best to work *lighter* in tone than required and gradually build up when using dye.

By letting the dye dry in the saucer before using it, it is less likely to sink into the emulsion, and can be wiped off readily when mistakes are made. For dealing with larger areas that need tone-strengthening by weak washes of dye, grey dye is available—this is in fact preferred by many for ordinary spotting instead of black. Brown can be obtained for use on warm-toned prints, and may be mixed with either black or grey if desired.

• • •

MAKING AN ALBUM

HOW DO YOU PRESENT your photographs? Do you make enlargements of various sizes and shapes, to be handed round to the company-at-large? Do you carry a set of contact prints in

Correct focusing is all-important (see 'Hints on focusing, page 88). Top left: Mis-judged distance setting (or too-close approach) can result in sharp background and fuzzy subject. Above: All-over sharpness due to depth-of-field being too great (lens aperture too small) making undesirable background compete with subject. Left: Differential focusing (page 89) keeps subject sharply recorded against unsharp, and thereby subdued, background. N.B. Brick walls are not normally acceptable backgrounds for portraits—one was used here to emphasize the out-of-focus effect.

An orange filter clarifies detail in distant views, gives strong sky effects, and increases contrasts in black-and-white pictures. Its over-correction can produce dramatic effects, but may give black 'empty' shadows when the prevailing light is in itself contrasty.

Animal pictures must be sharp, and show texture. Outdoors, medium-speed film is generally fast enough for all but the liveliest animals. Great patience is essential—and be prepared to shoot several frames.

TINSEL
GIFT RIBBON
For Attractive Presents
GUM
SOLUTION
Calendar

Calendar

A 2x or 3x yellow filter is a very useful 'general purpose' one for landscape studies with most black-and-white films (see page 88). The rendering of foliage and sky is acceptable, without over-correction.

Left. Making a calendar. (Top) The materials required (see page 120). (Centre) Attaching the date tab. (Bottom) The completed calendar.

Electronic flash is ideal for photographing animals indoors; most equipment is capable of 'freezing' quite fast movement. Avoid including too much furniture, patterned drapes etc., and have someone on hand to help you.

Left. Hoar frost makes practically everything look decorative (see page 63). Medium- and slow-speed films will produce better contrasts than the faster films, and slightly increasing the development time is often helpful.

Snow needs sunshine to reveal its brittle, powdery texture and modelling. Foreground expanses devoid of shadow are best avoided.

your wallet or pocket-book to produce at convenient times? Are your best efforts framed and displayed as wall pictures, or do you simply follow hide-bound convention and painstakingly put them into those familar dark-leaved albums by means of tiny gummed corner slips?

Whichever course you take, have you ever stopped to think *constructively* about it? Those hours of patient endeavour, composing, taking, developing, printing (to say nothing of maybe years of practical experience) are crystallized into that rectangle of bromide paper. Everything that has gone before was but a means to an end . . . the final pictorial print; it is surely well worthwhile going to a little extra trouble to make the most of your results?

There is a great deal of pleasure and satisfaction to be had from making up an album in true 'picture book' style, with a sense of continuity and subject-balance. Furthermore, it is easier than you think! First decide upon the overall dimensions; 10 x 8in. is very suitable, although of course you can depart from standard paper sizes if you wish. From the practical point of view, post-card size is probably the smallest advisable. The prints themselves, mounted back to back, form the pages, and can be of single or double weight paper—this is a matter of personal choice.

The cover

Next, choose your negatives. Here you must be ruthless and select only the best; one indifferent print can spoil the whole effect. The cover picture is particularly important: it needs to be something bold and simple, yet in keeping with the general contents of the album. It must also be such that a suitable title can be added without becoming too confused with the picture detail; intricate 'fussy' scenes are seldom suitable.

Try to arrange things so that individual pages do not clash with one another as regards subject, treatment, and picture-size. In other words: plan everything *before* you start printing. If you want to make your album landscape shape instead of upright, the white margins may be either at the left or right instead of at the top or bottom as shown in the illustration on page 72.

When making the prints, aim to get them as uniform as possible. Avoid putting dark, low-key subjects immediately opposite delicate-toned ones and so on; keep the actual print quality and depth consistent if you can. Then, when the album pages are opened, the contents appear as a properly-produced book. It is not essential to stick to one kind of paper surface throughout; a 'Royal' or semi-matt surface is recommended, but an occasional page on glossy or other surface can add to the general attraction. Use single or double weight paper according to the final bulk required.

The normal printing frame creates white margins which you will have to trim off, so if you want 10 x 8in. pages you must either work with 12 x 10in. paper or make a simple right-angled card guide (see page 186) to lay on the enlarger baseboard, to position the paper for margin-less prints. To ensure paper flatness in printing however, it is usually better to use a frame and then trim. Unless you are making a full-page print, broad masking will be needed at the bottom or top of the page. This is simply accomplished by putting a piece of cardboard over the part left uncovered by the printing frame's adjustable arms.

Straightforward arrangement

Don't have *all* margins at the base; some prints may look well with plenty of top margin. Composition and proportions will also influence this. The main thing is not to introduce 'arty' shapes; tasteful, straightforward arrangement is far better. Although it is possible to have more than one picture per page, this requires careful, accurate masking, and even more careful printing in order to match tones and quality in each. For a start, at least, it is wiser to play safe and keep to one.

The finished prints are mounted back to back with rubber mountant ('Cow') or dry mounting tissue; the former is more flexible. Here again, you must work carefully; those edges will split open unless extra attention is given to them, or you may find that slight inaccuracies in trimming have produced off-square edges when you try to pair off the pages. Alternatively, you can get the mounting done commercially and trim the pages afterwards.

Now comes the tricky part—the lettering. This must be neat and well-executed in a plain style with a single-stroke pen; if you doubt your capabilities in this direction, wording can be typed on a gummed slip, or the pages left untitled. Avoid lengthy captions and heavy, large letters; correct spacing is important too.

Fortunately, the cover title is an easier proposition, thanks to the useful 'Letraset' transfer alphabets. With these, the choice of style and size is considerable, and you simply apply your wording letter-by-letter, transfer-fashion, to achieve a perfect printers' type title. The lettering should be added after you have mounted your cover print on mounting board to make a substantial outer, a final touch being a sheet of clear celluloid or acetate—this also keeps the cover clean.

Lastly, there's the binding. Wholesale bookbinders will usually do this for you, in wire ('Spirax') or plastic; but send a letter of enquiry first, stating your requirements and thickness of the album, in case the firm does not possess machinery capable of handling that size. Remember to do all your spotting and hand-work before binding, and if you must use 'dope' on any of the prints, use it very sparingly or you may find it coming off on the opposite page, giving a patchy effect.

• • •

MAKING A 'CONTACT' BOOK

UNLESS SOME FORM of filing system is employed by the user of 35mm. film, as time goes on it becomes impossible to avoid getting into a hopeless muddle. Many people file their contact prints in strip form together with the corresponding negatives, but this method has its drawbacks: in theory, one inserted the contact-strip face outwards, with the negative strip immediately behind, in a transparent film-wallet or pocket in the page of an album. In this way the prints could be viewed without disturbing either negative or contact-strips.

In practice, unfortunately, one nearly always had to draw out the contact-strip to allow for critical examination of the tiny prints. Continually sliding these strips in and out becomes a source of danger to the negative stored with it—minute scratches can occur, and while locating any particular print in the dark-room there is a risk of negatives dropping on to the floor.

By making yourself a 'contact' book (a separate container in which all contact prints are systematically filed) you will find that the advantages it offers greatly outweigh any trouble involved in the making.

Preparing the book

From a stationer's, procure a fairly thick and strong book, of foolscap or quarto size, and remove alternate pages by cutting them about a quarter of an inch from the centre binding. Don't tear them out, or the rest of the pages will eventually fall out as well; a simple way to remove them is to use a sharp knife or razor blade and only cut half-way through the paper with a quick and light pressure (this is not difficult to do). By gently pulling, it will divide at the cut, and there is no fear of the adjoining page being accidently cut through and weakened. Unless alternate pages are removed, the book will bulge and break as it is filled with prints.

Now, instead of keeping your contact prints in strip form, it is more convenient to lay the negative strips side by side on a sheet of 10 x 8in. bromide paper, put a sheet of glass on top, and expose it to the enlarger light after having made a trial test-strip. Five strips of six negatives are comfortably accommodated by a 10 x 8in. sheet, the remaining six can be put on a small slip of bromide paper. These prints are then stuck on to successive pages of the book; a foolscap-size page will hold 36 prints if close-trimmed, and it is better to use only one side of the pages if possible. 'Cow' rubber adhesive is very suitable.

Unless you have your own pet method of filing and reference, the following will be found reliable and convenient: negatives are filed in consecutively numbered film wallets, and stored in a strong box, card-index fashion; this film reference number is also written on the page of the book bearing the corresponding contact print. Pertinent data or details concerning particular shots can also be written on the page, or on the blank page immediately opposite the contact print.

Working routine

When you wish to make an enlargement from any print in the book, it is the work of a moment to find the appropriate negative. For example, it might be 'exposure No. 14 in wallet No. 58' etc.;

the system is completed by writing the reference numbers on the back of each enlargement when it is made—in this case it could be shortened to '14/W58' or 'W58/14' as you wish. Any further copies which may be required at a future date are thus easily repeated.

If you use bulk 35mm. film, the exposures should be numbered before cutting the developed negatives into strips. Write the numbers directly on to the negatives with a fine mapping-pen or similar nib, using Indian ink.

• • •

THE PERFECT BUTT-JOINT

IN MAKING UP composite enlargements such as panoramas, where two or more prints must be accurately joined to present a wide vista, careful, patient technique is necessary to achieve success. As a rule, single-weight paper is used, and the over-

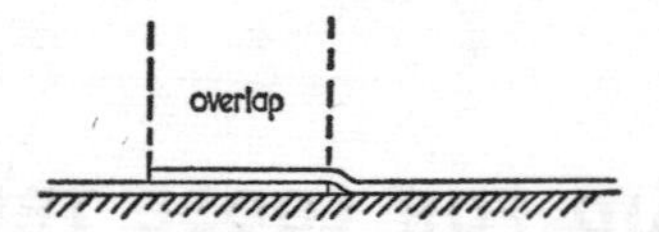

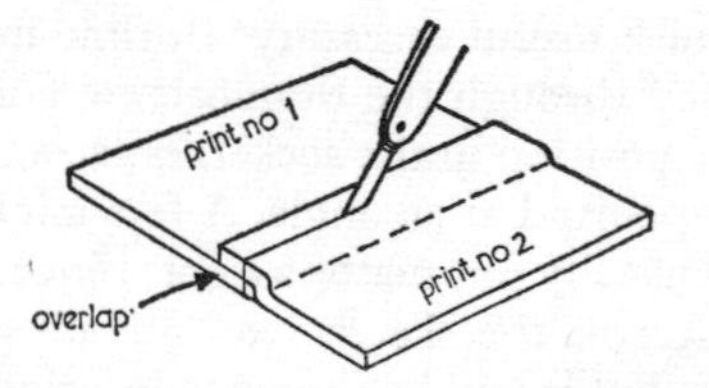

lapping edges of the prints are scraped or rubbed down with fine sandpaper to reduce thickness and thus make the joining edge less noticeable. But even when this is carried out very carefully, if the overlap is straight and does not follow the outlines of any object, such as a building, figure or something similar, this join is still fairly obvious. It is in cases like this, when a straight join must be made, that the following method will be found to be by far the most effective.

Print No. 1 is mounted in position with rubber mountant, lightly squeegeeing into contact with a roller. Print No. 2 is then meticulously registered with an overlap as shown (exaggerated for the sake of clarity) and the roller lightly mounting it to prevent slip. Next, a steel straight-edge is placed roughly midway between the overlapping edges, and the two prints are cut through with a very sharp knife. A firm but not too hard pressure will enable this to be done *without penetrating the mount*; this is by no means as difficult to do as it seems.

Both the unwanted trimmings are immediately removed, the edge of print No. 2 being gently peeled back to allow for this, then replaced, and any surplus rubber mountant on the surface rubbed off with the fingers. The two cut edges should now form a perfect, virtually indetectable, butt-joint on the mount when given final pressure from the roller. This procedure is also useful for joining prints for photo-murals etc.

• • •

FIRST AID FOR LOOSE TRIPOD HEADS

THE POPULAR TYPE of metal collapsible tripod with ball-and-socket head is a most useful accessory. In time however, trouble may be experienced through the thumbscrew failing to lock the ball head firmly in position in the socket, especially when a heavy camera is to be supported at an angle. A few minutes' work with a screwdriver will usually put matters right. Since different makes vary slightly in design, the sketch may not illustrate your particular one exactly, but it will be the same in principle.

When you tighten the thumbscrew, its pointed end forces the moulded block upwards, which in turn holds the ball head tightly against the casing. If you undo this casing you will find that the place where the screw meets the block has become indented and worn, thus the screw cannot exercise pressure at this point. By the very simple expedient of slightly rotating the block so that a fresh unworn section falls immediately opposite the screw end, the screw can once again function satisfactorily.

Doing this each time it wears loose will greatly extend the working life of the tripod head, as the block can be moved many

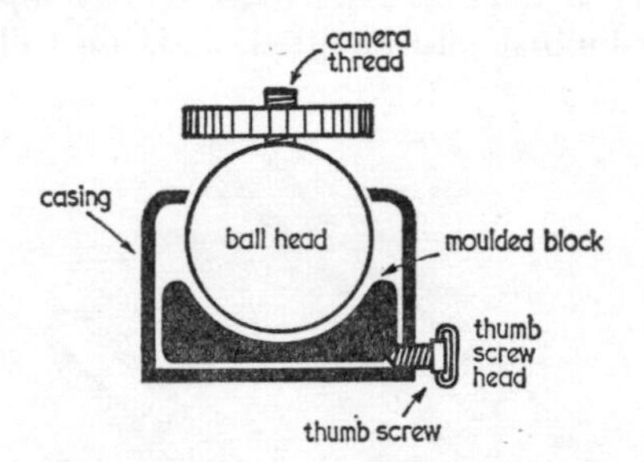

times before it becomes worn all round the circumference. Sometimes it happens that the screw has become too worn to penetrate sufficiently to contact the block. Then the only remedy is to have a new screw cut if possible—not a difficult job for anyone who has access to a screw-cutting lathe. Or as a last resource, file away the inner surface of the thumbscrew head just enough to let the screw make internal contact once more.

• • •

HANDY 'SPOT' TORCH

DURING A SLIDE SHOW, if often happens that you may wish to refer to notes on certain transparencies, or locate one particular slide quickly; switching on a table lamp to do this can be distracting to your audience, besides flooding the room with unwanted light. An ordinary pocket torch is frequently used, but even this can prove to be unneccessarily bright. A few minutes' work adapting a 'fountain pen' type of torch will be found to be well worth while; the sketch shows how it is done.

The torch is given an 'extension tube' of black paper, fastened with two or three bands of *sellotape* or ordinary gummed strip, and as an extra refinement, the torch bulb can be blacked over with black enamel or some opaque medium, leaving a little clear spot about an eighth of an inch in diameter. The paper tube should be about six inches long, and should be rolled tightly round the body of the torch otherwise it may slip off. For best results, a spot-bulb should be fitted, and you will find that the

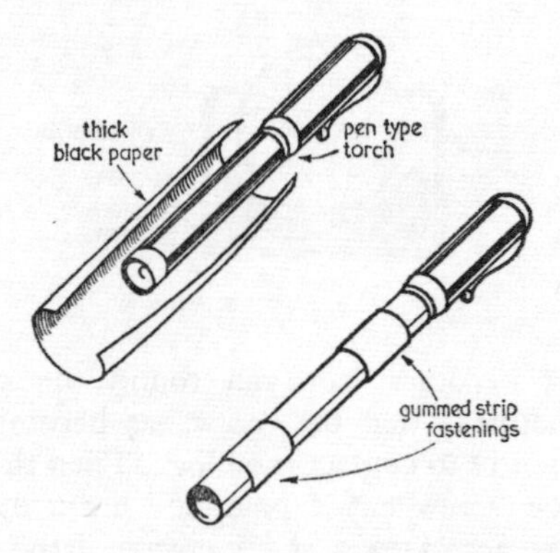

torch will now give a small disc of light that you can direct onto your notes, slides etc, without trouble.

In addition, this hooded torch can be used to 'paint with light' during the making of an enlargement. By 'chasing' the spot of light around the sky area, an otherwise blank sky can be given tone to take off the whiteness; to do this effectively, a little trial-and-error routine is needed. The important thing to remember is that the light must be kept moving all the time, or patchiness will result. For darkening really small areas in this manner, the end of the tube may be covered with a small cone of black paper with a hole in the apex.

If it is found on development that the darkening is insufficient, the treatment can be repeated before rinsing and fixing the print. In the case of skies, the trick is to get a smooth graduated tone.

• • •

COPYING ARM FOR AN ENLARGER

A COPYING ARM for use on a vertical enlarger is a very useful accessory, not only for its fundamental purpose of copying manuscripts, typescript, illustrations etc., but also for photographing small objects such as insects, coins, stamps and the like. From the accompanying sketch an efficient arm can be made quite simply and cheaply, the dimensions will depend upon the enlarger for which it is intended; basically, it should be constructed so that when your camera is in position in the front cradle, its lens should be approximately over the centre of the baseboard. Adapting the design of the arm to suit your equipment should present no difficulties.

In use, the arm fits on the upright column of the enlarger in

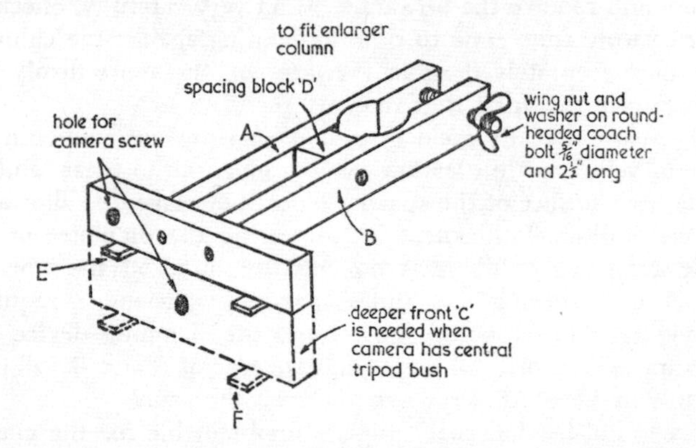

place of the lamphouse, the wing nut securing it at any desired height from the baseboard. By means of a camera-retaining screw (not shown, but readily obtainable from most dealers) or threaded rod with wing nut, the camera is held against the face C so that it is parallel to the baseboard. Supplementary lenses or extension tubes are then fitted to the camera, thus enabling close-ups and extreme close-ups to be obtained by adjusting the height of the camera accordingly and focusing. Correct positioning of the object to be photographed (with non-reflex cameras) is facilitated by making a simple plumbline.

By standing the baseboard near the edge of a table and reversing the direction of the arm so that the camera lens points towards the floor, quite large areas can be covered, this arrangement proving rather more convenient than employing a tripod. In these circumstances the supplementary lens or extension tubes can of course be dispensed with. The baseboard must be weighted down with heavy books or similar, or it may tip backwards due to the weight of the overhanging camera.

The copying arm is constructed from 1 x ½in. wood. To cut away the segments so that it grips the circular column of the enlarger, a curved chisel or pocket knife should be used. Having determined the diameter of this column, the spacing block D should be held tightly between the sides A and B and used as a centre for a compass to mark a circle of similar diameter (or slightly larger) in the appropriate position. Do this on top and bottom and remove the unwanted wood very carefully, checking the curvature from time to time by holding against the column. The more accurately these curves are cut, the more firmly will the arm grip the upright of the enlarger.

To ensure a really good grip, and also prevent scratching, a piece of velvet or thin leather may be glued on to these, and on to the back surface of the spacing block, but make due allowance for the additional thickness by increasing the diameter of the circle accordingly. There is no need to round-off the working surface of the spacing block unless maximum efficiency is required as long as it just touches the column the clamping device will function satisfactorily. A screw on each side of A and B will hold it firmly in place. All screws should be countersunk.

If a round-headed coach bolt is unobtainable for the clamp, two wing nuts with washers and a length of threaded rod will be equally effective. Tighten only just sufficiently to cause it to grip the column; further tightening may strain the arms. The position of the hole for the camera screw is dependent upon the location of the tripod bush on your camera base; if this is centrally-located, the front (C) of the wooden arm may have to be made from 2 x ½in. wood to prevent it fouling the sides A and B. Unnecessary tension on the camera screw is avoided by having two small supports E and F as shown—these also serve to keep the camera parallel to the enlarger baseboard. The supports can consist of metal strips or wood blocks screwed to the underside of C, again positioned to suit your particular camera. Properly made, this copying arm will give good service.

• • •

SIMPLE DISH WARMER

A SIMPLE BUT effective dish warmer can be easily made from an ordinary biscuit tin, by cutting a hole in one side to take a lamp holder as shown in the sketch. Make sure the electrical connections are safe, and as an extra precaution, the tin should

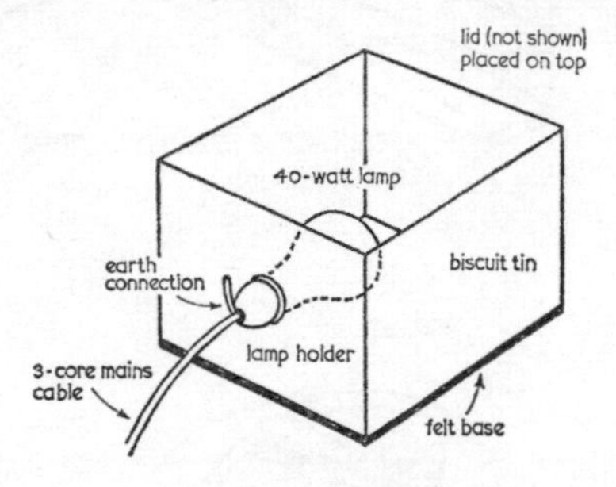

be 'earthed' by means of triple-cored cable—a spot of solder or a small nut and bolt adjacent will secure the third wire to the tin. All that remains is to put a 40-watt lamp in the holder and replace the lid. If you find there is light-leak from the edges of the lid, this can be cured by sealing with a length of insulating tape to close the gap. In the ordinary way, there is no likelihood of over-heating occuring, and a 10 x 8in. or even a 12 x 10in. dish can be kept satisfactorily warm when placed on top, except in very cold conditions. An additional refinement can be achieved by covering the base of the tin with felt or similar material to conserve heat, and also prevent possible scratching or marking of the surface on which it is placed.

• • •

DIFFUSERS FOR PHOTOFLOODS

A PHOTOFLOOD LAMP in its metal reflector gives a directional and 'hard' light that makes for contrasty results in portraiture, especially when used in the average living-room, where it cannot be placed far from the sitter. Softer, and more pleasing effects

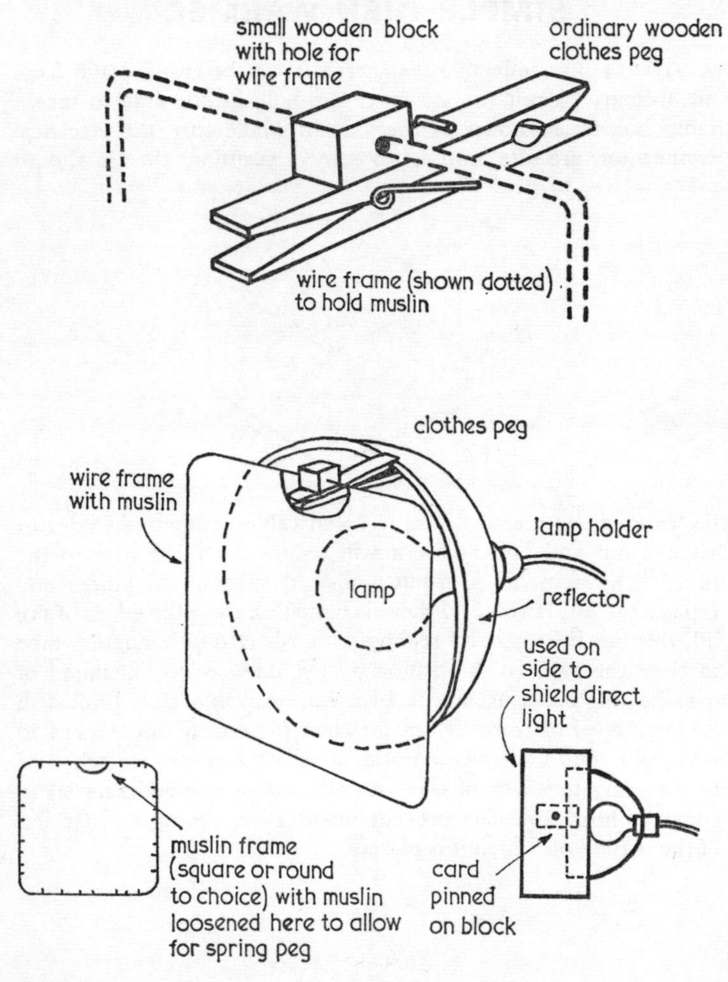

can be achieved by putting a diffusing screen in front of the lamp, thereby spreading the light and making contrasts more manageable. But a photoflood gets very hot, so merely draping its reflector with muslin or similar material can cause scorching.

To lessen the risk of this happening (provided it is not left in place for long periods) the muslin can be stretched across a wire frame—rectangular or circular in shape—and supported by means of an ordinary wooden clothes' peg to clip on the rim of the reflector. As the drawing shows, to do this, a small block of wood with a hole to take the wire frame must be fixed to the peg with adhesive such as *Evo-Stik.* If the hole is made so that the wire is a fairly tight fit, and the muslin shaped or loosened near the peg, the diffuser may then be swung upwards out of the way when not needed during a 'session', instead of being unclipped. When the *lamp is tilted upwards* however, an additional peg support should be used on the opposite edge to prevent the muslin dropping on the reflector at that point.

If desired, the small wooden block can be fixed at the *end* of the peg instead of the position shown; in this way the muslin is held even further from this lamp. This little gadget will also be found helpful for preventing direct rays from a lamp shining into the camera lens. A block of soft wood similarly fixed (without the wire frame attached) will allow a piece of cardboard to be pinned on to it; clipped to the appropriate side of the reflector it then forms an effective shield or 'blinker'.

Another type of diffuser may be made from the lid of a tin (one

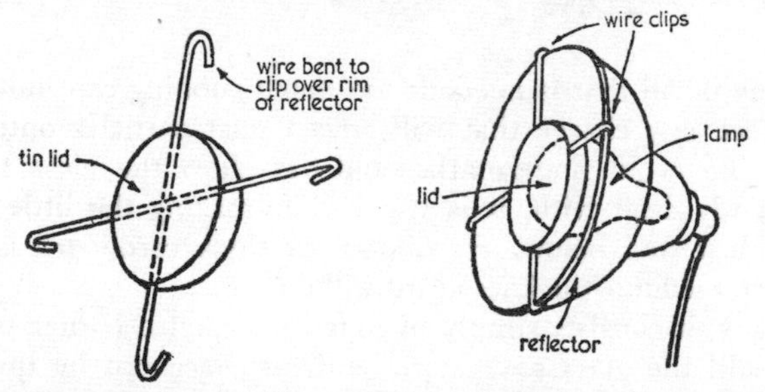

about three inches in diameter is suitable) and two lengths of $\frac{1}{8}$in. tinned copper wire. Four holes are drilled close to the top of the lid to take the wire, which is pushed through as shown to make a good tight fit. If there is looseness, slight bending of the uppermost wire may remedy it, overwise soldering will overcome the trouble. The tin is centred over the lamp in its reflector, and the ends of the wire are then bent to fit over the rim—here again there must be no slipping, or the diffuser may fall off when the lamp is tilted.

• • •

CLEANING AID FOR SLIDE GLASSES

ALTHOUGH MOST cover glasses for colour slides are factory-cleaned, it is usually advisable to give them a final clean before actually assembling a slide. A light rub over with a soft, lintless

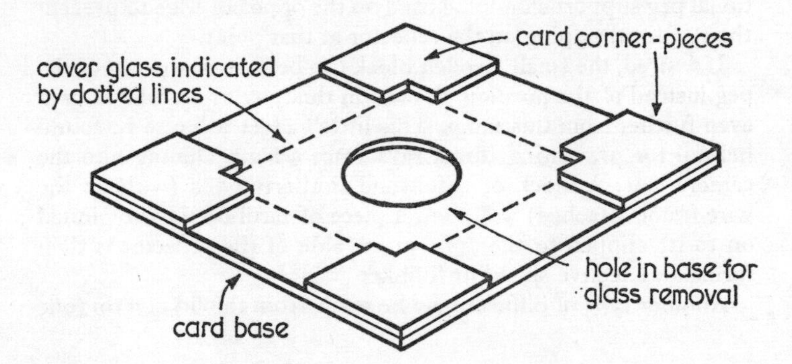

cloth may be all that is needed; too much rubbing can induce a static electricity charge that will attract dust particles onto the surface. To avoid fingermarks, and yet allow the glass to be conveniently dealt with, it is worthwhile making the little card holder illustrated below. Hardboard or thick cardboard is not necessary, medium-thickness card will do.

Basically, it consists simply of four right-angled corner-pieces which hold the glass so that its entire surface can be quickly cleaned; the centre hole in the base facilitates removal of the glass afterwards—although in fact there is no point in making the corners a tight fit. On the other hand, too much 'play' or looseness is undesirable. For speedy construction, on old cover glass can be laid over the hole in the card base, and the four corner-pieces stuck into place round it; finally, the outer edges of the holder can then be trimmed to suit. Leave sufficient margins for comfortable handling.

• • •

PICTURE-MASKING AID

YOU WILL FIND that two L-shaped pieces of matt black showcard (or even the black paper or wrapping used for bromide paper) can prove extremely useful when composing a picture from the projected image on the baseboard during enlarging. By sliding both at right-angles over the picture area until a satis-

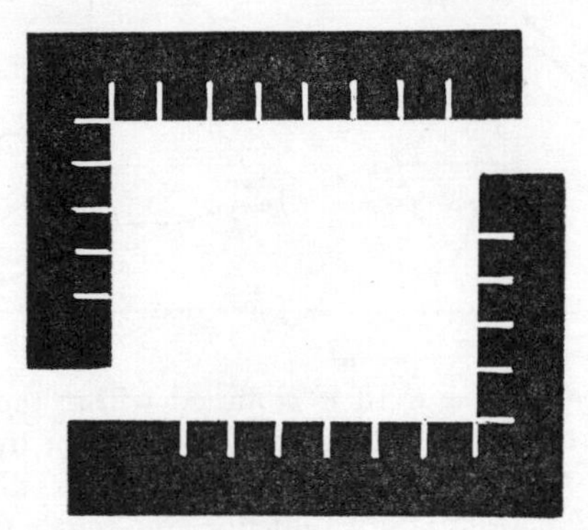

factory result is arrived at in the rectangle they enclose, the process of masking or 'selective enlarging' is speeded up. Doing the same thing with a printing frame involves adjustment and re-adjustment of the sliding arms.

If the inner edges of the cards are marked in inches with white ink, process white or similar, this will help you in your choice of paper size too. Once the picture-area is decided, the printing frame can be adjusted accordingly. The cards may also be used to ascertain the cropping of a print—usually white ones are advocated, but in practice black is equally effective. A *width* of

2in. is suggested for the 'arms' of the cards; length can vary to suit requirements.

In order to get sufficient viewing distance for such cropping, it may be helpful (in the case of enlargements of 10 x 8) or more) to put the print on the floor. Alternatively, you might like to invest in a 'diminishing glass'—which is a sort of magnifier-in-reverse. This is a useful aid to composition sometimes used by artists.

A NOVEL 'DODGER'

ALTHOUGH IT IS customary to use a card with a small hole in the centre of it, for carefully 'dodging' about the projected image and so giving areas extra exposure when enlarging, sometimes a certain amount of light-spill occurs. By using a cone made of

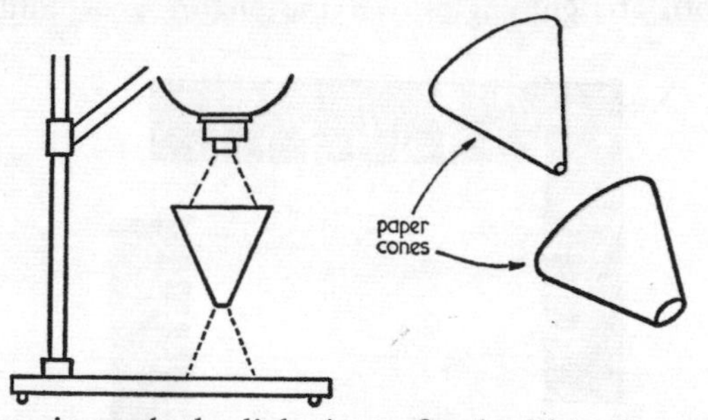

black paper instead, the light is confined within the cone, apart from a small circle of light which emerges from the tip. It is worth while making two or three such cones with different-sized openings; manipulation is not difficult, and considerable control can be achieved with a little practice.

If desired, a short length of wire can be bent to a circular shape at one end to hold the cones; this will facilitate handling. A small jam jar (or similar container) will serve as a 'former' round which to bend the wire.

IMPROVING PRINT FORCEPS

PRINT FORCEPS occasionally scratch or abraid the surface of a wet print. To overcome this, and at the same time improve the

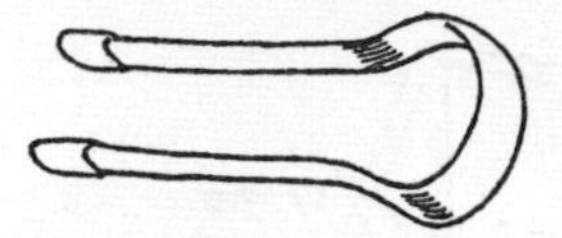

gripping powers of the forceps, cover the ends with fingertips cut from an old rubber glove. An adhesive such as *Evo-Stik* or 'Bostik' will secure them firmly in position.

Over a period of time, most forceps tend to become less springy. With those of stainless steel, it is a simple matter to remedy this by bending them outwards, but great care must be exercised with plastic ones or they will snap.

FOR NON-SLIP SHELVES

TO PREVENT BOTTLES or containers slipping off a crowded darkroom shelf, slit a length of rubber garden hose lengthwise (this is best done by means of an old pair of scissors) and slip it over the front edge of the shelf. The tension of the hose

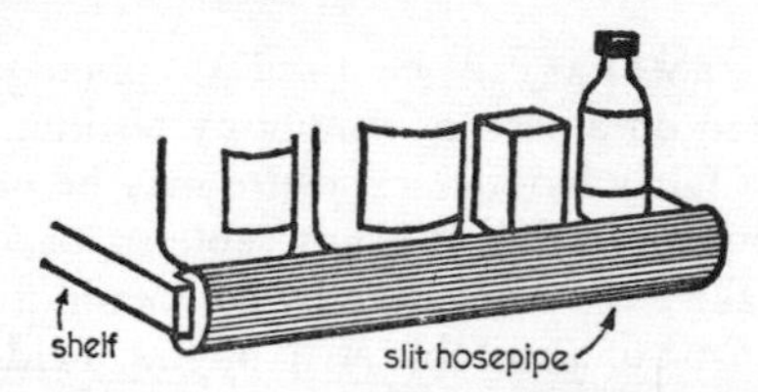

will usually keep it in place; if not, a tack or two will hold it. As an alternative (though not so effective) method, attach a strip of foam rubber draught-proofing, sticking this on the top edge.

It is easier to keep shelves clean if they are painted with high-gloss paint—a wipe with a damp cloth will remove any spilt chemicals, whereas plain wood will absorb them. You may pre-prefer to cover the shelves with 'Fablon' or similar material instead.

USEFUL PRINT WASHER

PRINTS CAN BE washed in an ordinary sink by attaching a hosepipe to the tap, and holding it in position by clamp and string or spring clip, so that the end is along one side of the sink. Arrange things to obtain a jet of water that keeps the prints circulating gently, and fit an inexpensive drainer. Too much

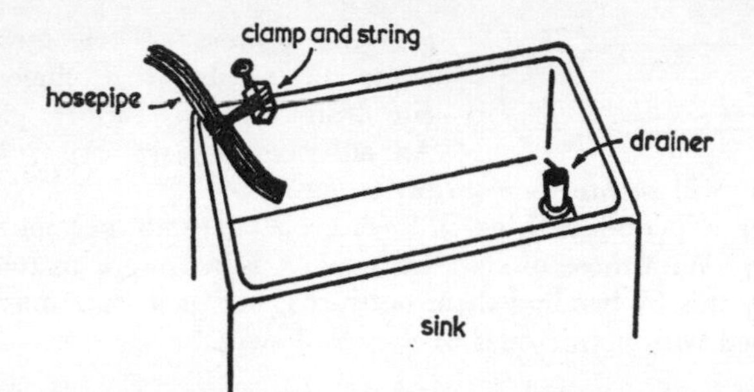

water pressure may damage the corners of the prints as they are whirled against the sides, too little will not keep them moving.

BROMIDE PRINTS FROM COLOUR TRANSPARENCIES

ALMOST ANY CAMERA can be used to photograph a transparency projected on a screen, simply by positioning it near the projector; but a fairly lengthy exposure may be needed with the medium- or slow-speed film it is advisable to load with. A better method is to make a copy negative by contact in a printing frame—which can consist of a suitable strip of glass held tightly against a similar strip of plywood by means of spring clips. Those whose cameras have interchangeable lenses, and which will therefore take extension tubes, may like to construct a copying device on the lines of the one shown in the drawing.

This gadget allows any filter to be used on the camera lens if desired, and even transparencies with marked colour-casts can often yield acceptable black-and-white prints. The distance from camera to transparency should be that applicable to the extension tube in use, details about this are normally given by the manufacturer; the distances of the opal glass and photoflood lamp are not critical. To ensure correct positioning of the camera, a wooden strip or 'stop' is provided; it is not *essential* to secure it with a threaded rod and wing nut screwed into the tripod bush (another stop at right-angles can be fitted instead) but it does make for easier working.

The hinged box which holds the transparency in grooves at its end, can be made of hardboard, plywood, or thick strawboard; so long as the transparency grooves are accurately aligned to be square-on at the correct distance, all should be well. In practice, it will be found that a 1:1½ extension tube is more convenient than a same-size (1:1) tube, because it gives margins that ensure that no edge of the transparency is cut off. Also, the hinged box protects the lens from extraneous light and unwanted reflections;

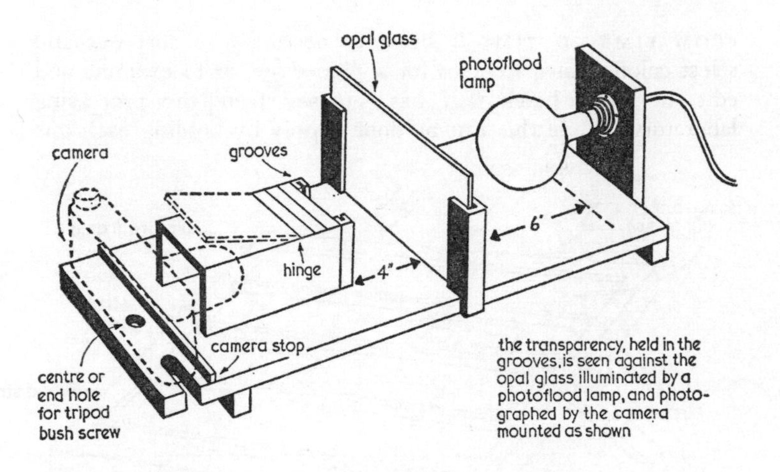

it should be painted matt black inside The illumination is from a photoflood lamp behind a screen of opal glass, against which the camera 'sees' the transparency.

With the lamp switched on and a transparency in place, many exposure meters will give a reading from the camera position, but generally speaking it is better to make a few trial exposures—consistently correct exposures should follow. Medium-speed film is suitable. Try to arrange things so that thin (slightly over-exposed) colours are not recorded on the same film-length as those of the denser and more contrasty variety, otherwise trouble might be experienced when developing the negatives due to these differences in contrast.

In choosing transparencies for photographing, make sure that the intended picture will be suitable for monochrome reproduction; in particular, do not expect good results when it is difference in tint rather than difference in brightness that provides the contrast between subject and background. Differences in brightness will be recorded on the negative, but a distinction due to tint only will very largely be lost unless accentuated by a suitably chosen filter.

VIEWING DESK FOR TRANSPARENCIES

FROM TIME TO TIME it becomes necessary to sort out and select colour transparencies for a slide show, or to examine and edit the latest batch that has returned from the processing laboratory. While this can be done simply by holding each one

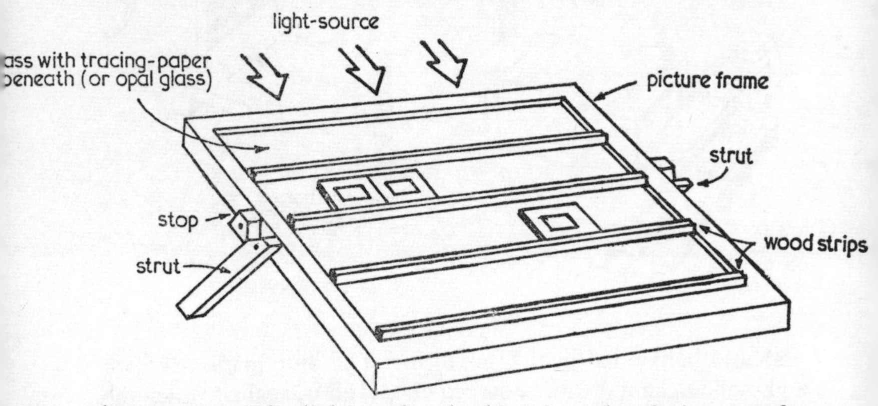

in turn up to the light, or by checking in a hand-viewer, a far better plan is to use some form of viewing-desk, with which twenty or more transparencies (according to size) can be inspected *en masse.*

An effective viewing desk can easily be constructed from an old picture-frame as follows: remove the back and glass, and screw wooden struts on the sides, using washers so that they can swivel to tilt the frame *face downwards* at about 45°. Small stops or screws should be positioned to fix the limit of travel of the struts, so as to prevent them closing down during use, and also to increase rigidity.

Next, cut a piece of thin tracing-paper so that its dimensions exceed those of the glass by roughly $\frac{1}{4}$in. in length and width.

Having thoroughly cleaned the glass, lay it in place on the paper to give equal margins all round, and drop both into the frame carefully so that glass and paper make a good fit round the sides—the paper should thus be pulled taut without folds or wrinkles forming. A few thin 'picture pins' may be tacked into the inner edges of the frame to secure this if desired, but are not essential.

Using 'Durafix' or similar adhesive, narrow strips of wood, hardboard or moulding are then stuck on the glass to serve as ledges to take the transparencies. For 2 x 2in. slides, a spacing of about $2\frac{1}{4}$in. between the strips will do, and the size of the glass should preferably be such that at least 20 slides can be comfortably accommodated. Crowding in too many by overlapping will hamper sorting, and thereby defeat the whole purpose of the desk.

In use, it should be stood upon a piece of white paper (or cloth) on a table close to a window or directly towards a light-source, so that the slides are evenly illuminated by light reflected from the paper. Silver paper, metal foil, or a mirror will provide brighter reflected light than white paper, but it is of a more directional nature. A whole series of slides may now be viewed in comfort. If and when the tracing paper becomes soiled or damaged, it is the work of a moment to replace it with a fresh sheet. Alternatively, a sheet of opal glass or translucent white plastic may be substituted for it. The viewing desk will also be useful when registering masks and transparencies for binding between cover glasses.

• • •

HANDY FLAT SQUEEGEE

THOSE WHO PREFER to use a flat squeegee rather than a roller when glazing prints, can make one from rubber draught-excluding strip. This, although tubular instead of the customary flat strip, functions equally well in practice, and with moderate care will last a long time. The wood for the handle should be about $\frac{1}{2}$in. to $\frac{5}{8}$in. thick, 2in. wide, and the length is dependent upon requirements; in most cases 6in. or 8in. will be sufficient. A slot is made in one edge, into which the flat portion of the rubber strip is fitted; it can be cut with a thick saw blade, and should be deep enough to reach further than the rubber strip when in position, as shown in the sectional sketch.

The edges of the slot are next grooved with a round rasp—the diameter of the tubular portion of the rubber strip governs the contour of the groove; then the outer edges of the wooden handle are slightly chamfered to prevent them coming into contact with the back of the print when the squeegee is used. Fine sandpaper

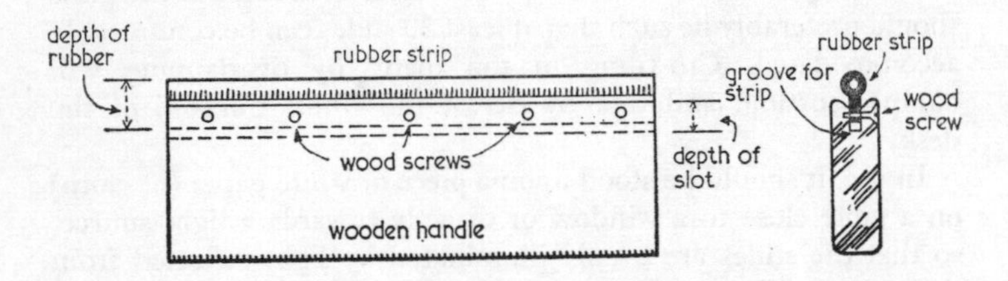

will give a smooth finish. By similarly rounding-off the holding-edge of the handle, a more comfortable grip is achieved.

Cut off the requisite length of draught-excluder strip and push the flat edge into the handle groove; small countersunk wood-screws will force the wood together at the two sides of the slot, and thus securely hold the rubber strip along its whole length. A coat of varnish on the wood is optional, but does help to minimize any bending or warping tendencies that might arise through the wood getting wet.

• • •

MAKING A SPOTLIGHT

A SPOTLIGHT IS A most useful piece of equipment for accentuating selected areas in portraiture, or for producing special effects with any lighting set-up. The main casing can be either a tin or a wooden box, adapted to hold a sliding support for the lamp, and fitted with a plano-convex condenser at the front end. Details for a simple spotlight are given in the drawing, with suggested dimensions for the wooden box; these however can be modified to suit the materials on hand if desired.

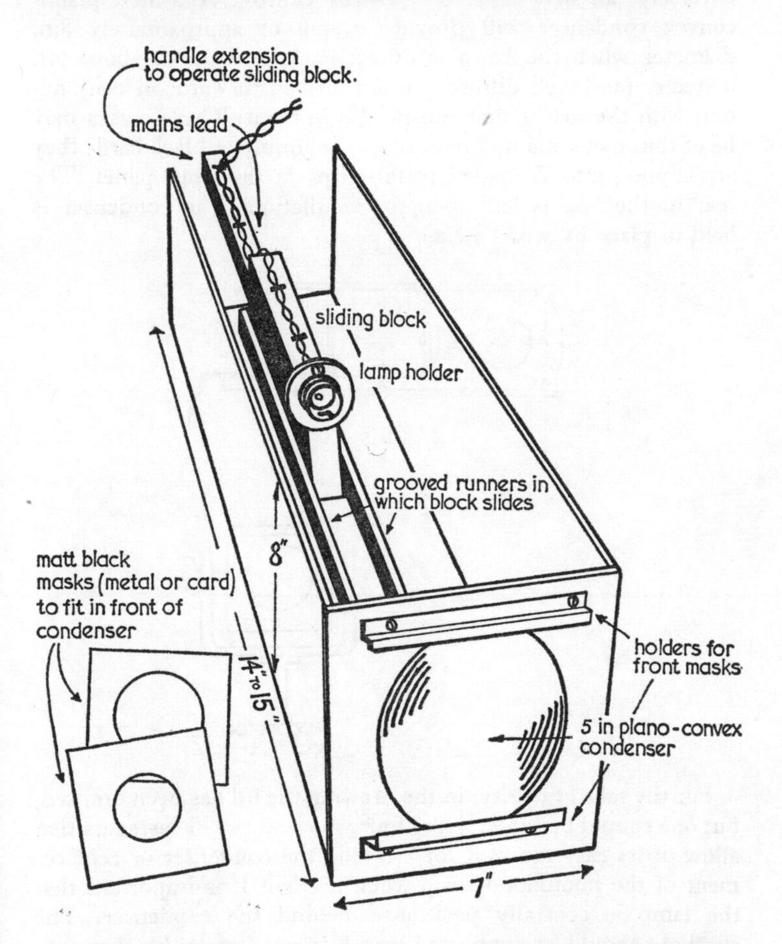

The photoflood lamp is supported on a block of wood sliding between two grooved wooden runners (some may like to adapt brass curtain runners instead) so that its distance from the condenser can be altered to produce 'spots' of varying diameters and intensity. For efficient working, the sliding action must be positive and smooth; a loose, wobbly support is unreliable, and coversely, an over-tight one lessens control. A 5-inch plano-convex condenser will provide a spot of approximately 8in. diameter when the lamp is drawn back, and up to about 6ft, diameter (and well diffused) when pushed forward, in conjunction with the masks that can be slid in front. These masks may be of thin metal painted matt black, or simply of black card; they are slipped into Z-shaped metal strips in the front panel. The rear of the box is left open for ventilation. The condenser is held in place by wood strips.

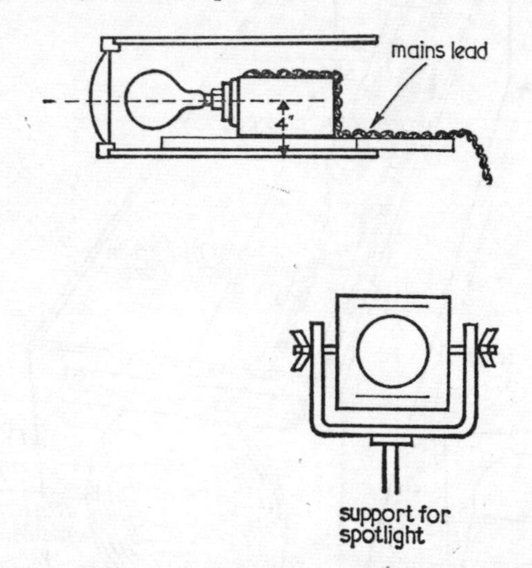

For the sake of clarity, in the drawing the lid has been omitted, but one should be fitted, using four wood-screws or fasteners that allow of its easy removal for cleaning the condenser or replacement of the photoflood lamp when needed. It is important that the lamp is centrally positioned behind the condenser. The spotlight should be supported by a U-shaped metal bracket with wing nuts to secure it at the required angle during use. A substantial tripod-type metal stand is also necessary—it is inadvisable to 'make-do' with some flimsy attachment to a light-weight collapsible camera tripod.

With a little modification, a smaller version can be constructed from two cylindrical tins or containers sliding one within the other. For example: using a 3in. plano-convex condenser fitted in one end of a tin about 4½in. diameter and 9in. in length, an inner tin approximately 3½in. diameter and 5in. or 6in. long would allow sufficient air-space between. The lamp could be accommodated in the smaller tin, the outer rim of which should have corks fixed to it to act as spacers, and to support it as it slides within the larger one.

The interiors must be painted with heat-proof matt black to prevent reflections, and a plastic handle attached to the outside to enable it to be moved and adjusted without burning the

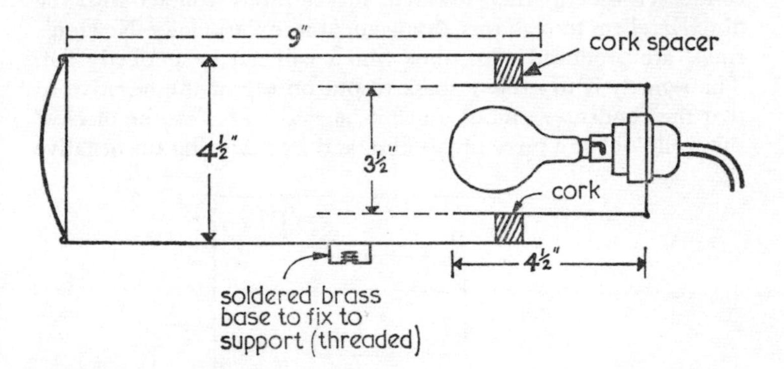

fingers—photofloods generate considerable heat! Again, to avoid over-heating, a through on/off switch should be incorporated in the mains lead, to switch off the lamp, which ought not to be left on for lengthy periods. This precaution should be observed with *any* form of home-made spotlight in the interests of safety.

It is a good idea to use a 60-watt or 100-watt ordinary household bulb when trying out a spotlight for the first time, to reduce heat and permit comfortable experimenting, changing over afterwards to a photoflood lamp when all is ready. In some cases, a 100-watt bulb may be all that is needed to throw light into a shadow area; but beware of mixing light-sources such as photofloods and household bulbs whenever you are photographing in colour. A spotlight will provide attractive top-lighting to form a 'halo' round the hair of a sitter, it can be used to cancel out unwanted cast shadows from other lamps, relieve plain backgrounds etc. For dramatic lighting, it can be the sole light-source if desired.

• • •

ENLARGING MASK

SOME ENLARGERS (such as the Leitz 'Valoy') hold the negative in place in the glassless carrier by means of a spring-loaded condenser which, when lowered, makes direct contact with the film. Excellent though this arrangement is, occasionally 'Newton's rings' are produced with films which will not lie perfectly flat. The remedy is to make a mask to put on top of the negative so that the condenser cannot touch its surface. This can be of clear thin celluloid or a piece of cut film, and by removing the negative

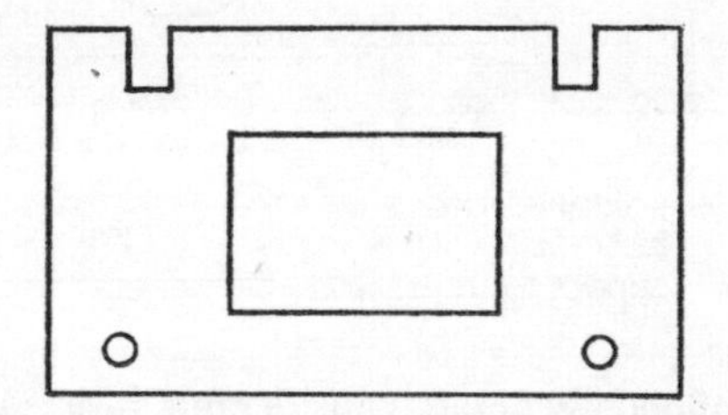

carrier and pressing it face down on the celluloid, sufficient indentation should result from the pins and guides to show where the holes and cut-outs must be made to clear them and allow the mask to lie flat. A sheet of carbon paper between the celluloid and the carrier will make the indentation clearer.

When the mask is in place, the central 'window' can be marked through from the back of the carrier with the point of a needle, and carefully cut out with a sharp knife and straight-edge. To ensure that none of the picture edges becomes shielded, this central cut-out should be made *very slightly larger* than that of the carrier; each edge and corner must be cleanly cut. If a piece of cut film is used, then the emulsion must be scraped off in the appropriate places to permit the negative numbers to be seen through the top and bottom slots of the carriers.

The finished mask is laid on top of a negative in the carrier, placed in the enlarger—and the lowered condenser now clamps the film all round the picture area, but not *on* it. Unless the film is buckled, or not properly dried out, Newton's rings should no longer be able to form.

● ● ●

BLACK BORDERS ON PRINTS

PICTORIAL PRINTS THAT have mainly light tones at or near the edges can often be improved by black borders. These have the effect of 'holding together' the compositional arrangement within, and the treatment is sometimes applied to exhibition pictures with marked success. The border can be added with Indian ink, using a pen or brush, but a much better way is to expose the edges of the bromide paper to the light from the enlarger, after printing but before development. This can be done by taking the paper out of the masking frame, placing a sheet of cardboard on top so that only one edge is uncovered, and switching on the lamp for about 8 to 10 seconds (without a negative in the carrier) for each edge in turn. Try to keep the borders equal in width, otherwise trimming will be needed afterwards. Upon development, the print should have rich black borders of even tone.

Alternatively, instead of using a sheet of cardboard, the outer envelope in which bromide paper is packed can be trimmed at one end and one side, so that the paper protrudes about ⅛in. from these edges. In this way *two* sides of the border are exposed simultaneously to the light, the procedure being repeated for the remaining two. Needless to say, the envelope must be carefully trimmed with a sharp knife and a straight-edge, if clean, uniformly accurate right-angled borders are to result. Individual envelopes will naturally be required for each size of paper used.

Yet another way is to make the little gadget shown in the sketch—place the pencil point along one of the inner edges of the masking board arms, switch on the torch and simply 'draw' it round the print area. This has the advantage of producing a narrow dark border within the normal white one. To construct it, a length of about 2in. is cut off the end of a soft 3B or 4B pencil, and the lead pushed out to leave a clean hole (the softer the pencil, the larger the hole). The pointed end is then gently rubbed on to a piece of fine sandpaper, the pencil being held upright to ensure a smooth square-cut opening which will not scratch the bromide paper surface.

Next, the flat end of the pencil is glued to a disc cut from stout card; a hole is pierced in the disc to match that in the

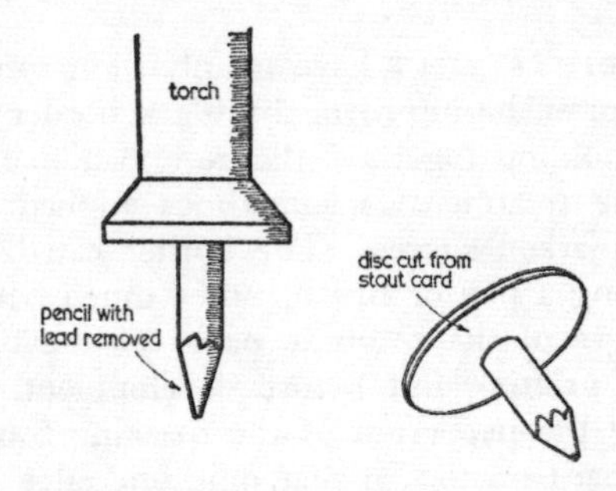

pencil, and the gadget is fitted to a small torch, in place of the glass. Again, take care to hold the pencil in an upright position when using, and remember to switch off the torch before you lift it from the paper!

• • •

GUARD FOR FLASH SYNCHRONISATION LEVER

UNLESS ONE IS careful to check regularly, the MX flash setting lever on some Compur and Compur type shutters can easily be moved to the wrong setting accidentally while the camera is in use. This of course, can lead to failures through incorrect synchronisation, as some may have found to their cost. An effective guard which will prevent the lever moving from either of the settings normally used, can be made from a thin strip of brass or aluminium.

First, a paper template should be made, to ensure that the position of the lever-retaining slot in relation to the flash socket and/or other extrusions can be accurately located and marked on the metal strip for cutting. The finished guard should fit snugly, conforming to the shutter's perimeter, and its ends secured by

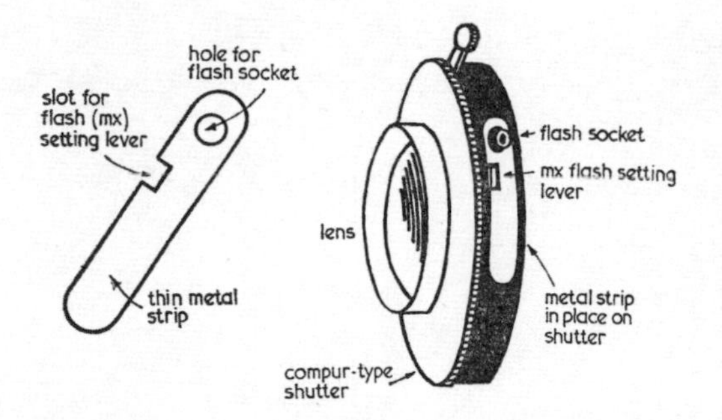

means of *Sellotape.* If desired, the strip can be painted black (matt or high gloss to choice) for a pleasing finish.

A more makeshift—but quite effective—means of keeping the flash lever in place, is to simply secure it with a piece of *Sellotape* only, peeling this off and replacing with new as and when necessary.

• • •

SAFETY LOCK FOR FLASH EXTENSIONS

A FLASH EXTENSION cable can be most useful, enabling a flash unit to be placed or held at some distance from the camera, instead of being mounted on the accessory shoe. However, there is sometimes a tendency for the connecting plugs to work loose and come apart during a shooting session, especially if the cable is well-used. Trying to tighten the plugs by squeezing them with pliers seldom succeeds, and can result in distorting the fittings and thus make subsequent connection difficult and unsatisfactory.

While it is possible to secure the plugs merely by binding with insulating tape or *Sellotape* after connecting, a more workmanlike job can be achieved by the addition of a small nut or collar that just slides over the outer connecting sleeve, and then locked in

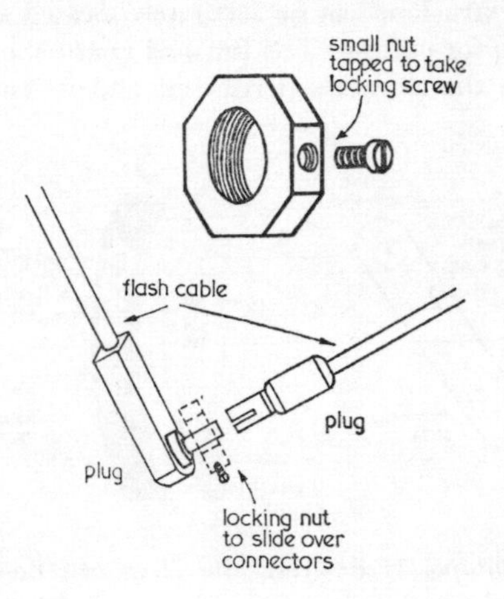

place by means of a screw. To take the locking screw, one side of the nut must be tapped (8 B.A. is suggested); the tightening action closes the outer split connector and causes it to grip the inner one without damage.

• • •

AN AUTOMATIC SIPHON

WHEN HYPO IS BEING washed out of prints it generally tends to remain at the bottom of the sink or dish; so efficient washing can seldom be achieved by merely placing prints under a running tap and allowing surplus water to flow over the edge of the dish or through the sink overflow. Some arrangement must therefore be made to draw the water off from the bottom, and suitable gadgets are available that fit into the sink outlet in place of the plug. Alternatively, you can easily make one from a rubber plug (the size to fit your sink) and a short length of rubber gas-tubing, ½in. diameter or thereabouts.

First, the ring and washers are removed from the plug with a pair of pliers, and the centre hole enlarged by cutting until one end of the tubing makes a tight fit. For permanence, the tube should be stuck in by means of rubber solution applied to the inside of the hole and the end of the tube—which should be pushed through until about half an inch projects. The other end

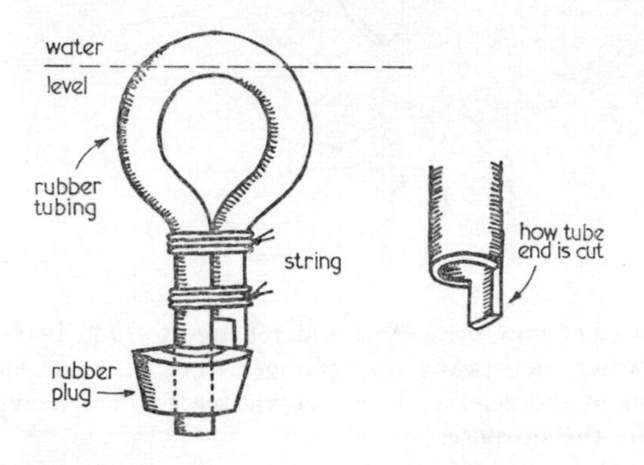

is cut to the shape shown, and the tube bent over and tied in position with string.

Next, rubber solution is freely applied along the parts of the tube which are in contact, and allowed to dry thoroughly; the string can then be removed. Placed in the sink outlet, it will be found that water will be automatically siphoned off without any adjustments being needed, and there are no working parts to go wrong.

• • •

IMPROVING A CABLE RELEASE

A BETTER, MORE comfortable grip can be provided on your camera's flexible cable release, by increasing the area of the shoulder' at the plunger end. This is easily accomplished by adding a suitably-sized washer (metal or plastic to choice) as shown, backed with a rubber grommet to keep it in place. A touch of *Evo-Stik* or similar adhesive will secure the grommet.

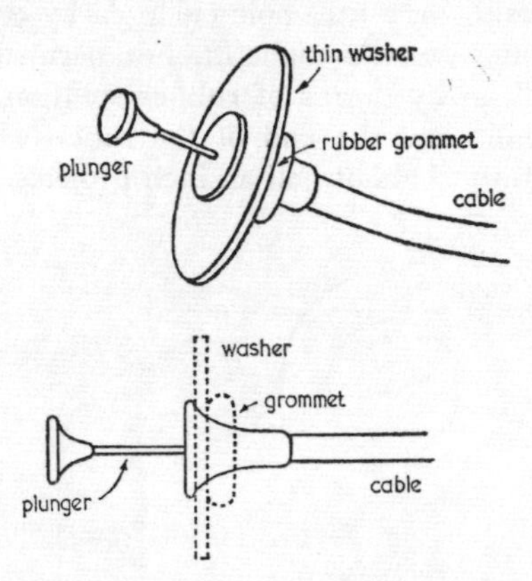

The washer now presents a wider flange to hold between the fingers when depressing the plunger, and thereby facilitates operation of the release. It is inadvisable to fit a heavy, thick washer for this purpose.

• • •

A LOW-LEVEL VIEWFINDER

THE OPTICAL DIRECT-VISION finder on miniature cameras is undoubtedly a most useful feature, but there are times when eye-level viewpoints are undesirable (as when photographing small children, animals, flowers etc.). For such subjects, low viewpoints are generally preferable, and although it is easy to stoop for waist-level shooting, to work lower than this may necessitate lying on the ground. A much more comfortable way of getting those really low viewpoints is to fit a meniscus-type 'brilliant' finder into the accessory shoe of the camera.

This kind of finder can be taken from an old folding camera, and it should not be difficult to get one from a market stall or junk shop for a small sum. Those on postcard-size or 3¼ x 2¼in. folding cameras are satisfactory for the purpose, their angles of view being approximately similar to the 50mm. and 45mm. lenses of 35mm. cameras. A suitable bracket can be made from brass, and soldered on to the finder so that it will slide into the accessory shoe.

The camera should now be put on a tripod, so that the bracket can be adjusted by slightly bending it until the meniscus finder corresponds with the direct-vision finder. It is usually best to set

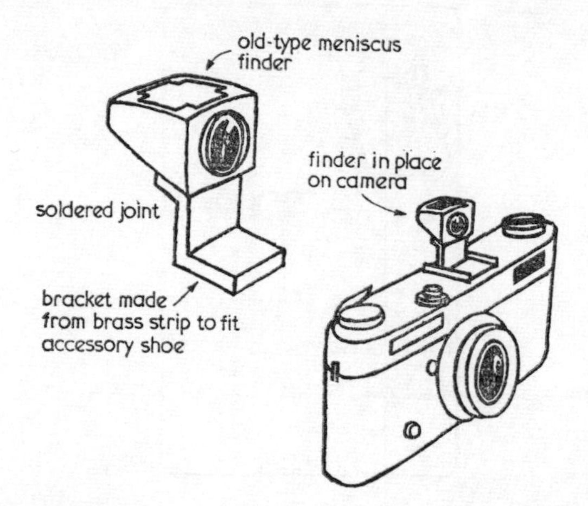

it for sighting at about 8 to 10 feet from the subject, since low-level viewpoints are unlikely to be needed at greater distances. Obviously, great accuracy cannot be expected, so it is advisable to allow fair margins round the picture area when shooting; also, remember to allow for parallax-error at closer distances.

• • •

A DARKROOM HOLD-ALL

SPACE LIMITATIONS OFTEN make it difficult to equip home darkrooms in the way one would like, and second-best arrangements have to be resorted to. Without sufficient shelving or cupboard facilities however, working routine can be disrupted at times. In such circumstances it is a good idea to hang a 'See-thru' shoe bag on the darkroom wall, to serve as a convenient hold-all for various items.

Costing only a few shillings and made of transparent plastic, it has twelve pockets (originally intended for shoes!) into which things such as print tongs, dodgers, focusing aids, dusters etc. can be individually slipped, ready for immediate use. Although

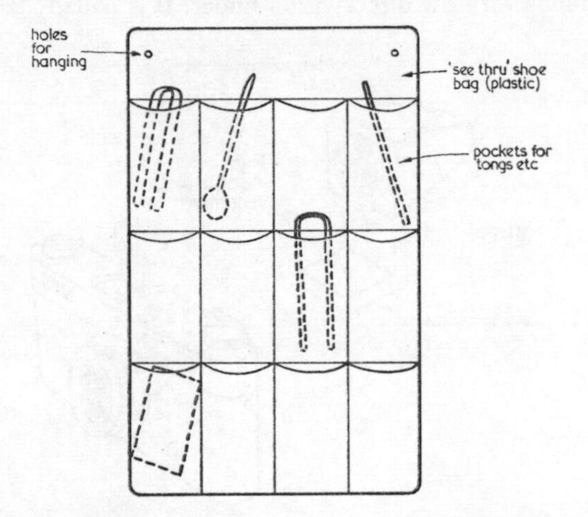

safely housed, each can then be seen at a glance and withdrawn as and when needed.

The shoe bag has eyeletted holes to facilitate hanging, and being made of plastic, is easily cleaned when necessary, and does not deposit stray fibres of material on the objects it accommodates, as a cloth bag would.

● ● ●

CARD GUIDE FOR BORDERLESS PRINTS

THE USUAL METHOD of obtaining borderless prints is simply to trim off the white borders that the masking frame produces.

There is much to be said for this, because the paper is held flat during printing. However, if at any time you should wish to make a print larger than your frame will accommodate, or want to utilize the full dimensions of the paper, it pays to construct a 'guide' so that you can accurately position the paper on the enlarger baseboard.

This can be made from stout card or hardboard of a suitable size; a scrap print can be used to ensure that the two locating strips are stuck on at right-angles if you have no set-square handy. The scrap print also serves as a white base upon which to focus

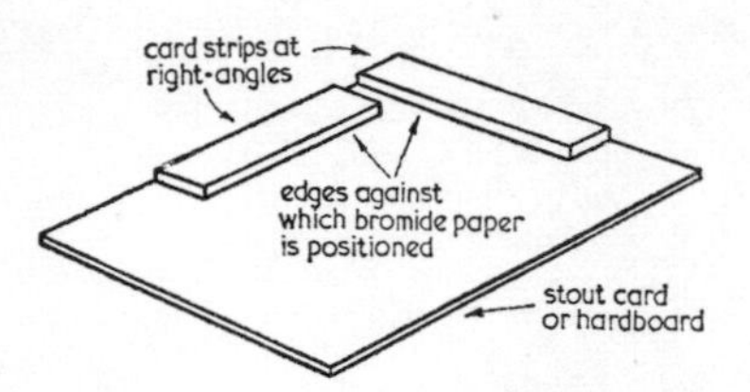

and compose your picture, replacing it with the bromide paper when all is ready. There is a risk of the bromide paper curling at the edges if exposures are lengthy, especially with single-weight paper. It is therefore often advisable to flatten each sheet first, by gently drawing it across the edge of the baseboard (face up!) to lessen this tendency.

The upturned lid of a cardboard box can be similarly used—that from a 10 x 8in. box for example being suitable for sizes up to wholeplate. By using the top and left-hand side to lay the paper against, the lid becomes a helpful guide.